EX LIBRIS

BILSTON ENAMELS
OF THE
18th CENTURY

by

TOM COPE

PUBLISHED BY THE BLACK COUNTRY SOCIETY

ISBN 0 904015 18 1

Acknowledgement of financial
aid to:—

The Metropolitan Borough of
    Wolverhampton.

Halcyon Days.

The Spaghetti Fund.

The enamels shown on the front cover and
frontispiece are reproduced by courtesy of
Wolverhampton Art Gallery and Museums,
Bantock House Museum.

Produced by Harold Parsons for the publishers, The Black Country
Society, 49 Victoria Road, Tipton, West Midlands and printed by
Reliance Printing Works, Halesowen, West Midlands.

FOR MARY

CONTENTS

SOURCES AND ABBREVIATIONS

SOURCES

Joseph Price, *An Historical Account of Bilston,* (1835).
George T. Lawley, *A History of Bilston,* (1893).
The Bilston Town Books and the Court Rolls of Stowheath Manor kept at the Staffordshire County Archives, William Salt Library.
The Bilston Registers, covering the period 1684 to 1746, published by the Staffordshire Parish Registers Society in 1937-38.
Wills, etc., which are kept at the Lichfield Record Office.
Trade Directories of Birmingham and the District for the period may be seen at Birmingham and Wolverhampton Reference Libraries.

ABBREVIATIONS

B.R.L., Bilston Reference Library.
Wolv. R.L., Wolverhampton Reference Library.
W.S.L., William Salt Library.
Sed. R.L., Sedgley Reference Library.
Birm. R.L., Birmingham Reference Library.
L.R.O., Lichfield Record Office.
Lawley, G. T. Lawley, *A History of Bilston,* 1893.
Price, J. Price, *An Historical Account of Bilston,* 1835.
S.R.S., Staffordshire Record Society.
T.E.C.C., Transactions of the English Ceramic Circle.

1

THE EARLY HISTORY OF BILSTON

TODAY Bilston is a town in the heart of the industrial Black Country and, having enjoyed independent status as town, Urban District and Borough, now finds itself absorbed into Wolverhampton County Borough which has itself become part of a huge metropolitan complex.

In this part of South Staffordshire there existed, from early times, small settlements scattered between woods, heath and moor. By the year 1000 A.D. hamlets had been established whose modern names indicate their ancient origin—Wednesfield, Wednesbury, Willenhall, Ettingshall and the chief one, Wulfruna's Heatun. Moreover the Lady Wulfrun had founded her religious settlement and 'Bilsetnatum' was part of the land granted in the Charter.[1]

When William I had his Domesday Survey made, we find 'Billestune' described as having '2 hides of land which is 4 caracates, and 8 villeins and 3 borderers with 3 ploughs. Also I acre of meadow land. The wood was about a furlong long and a half broad. It was worth 20 shillings and now 38 shillings '.[2]

The land had now come into the possession of the king, probably by an exchange, and remained so until the reign of Henry II who granted the woods and lands south of Wolverhampton, from time to time immemorial demesne of the Crown, comprising 3 hydes and 1 caracate, to one Roger Wascellan.[3] According to Lawley, it was returned to royal ownership in John's reign and an interesting entry in the Great Roll of his time states 'To Simon Fitzhubert of Billestune the king oweth 15 marks for six grey falcons '.[4]

Later it is recorded that Henry III granted the lands belonging to the Crown to Walter de Bilston for his valour at the battle

8

of Evesham in 1265, in which Simon de Montfort was killed.[5] Another appreciation of the fighting qualities of Bilston men, archers possibly, was made by Edward III for their services in France: 'We hereby declare all Bilston men, our most dutiful subjects, to be free from tolls, rents, wards, and courts, and all other customs of earthly servitude, throughout our realm, saving and excepting to our Majesty, from henceforth, in consideration of it being anciently a demesne of the Crown. To our valiant subject William de Bilston we entrust our sovereign will '.[6]

The area comprising Bilston was flat, yet there was higher ground to the west, and a clear stream, the Bilston brook, flowed eastwards to join the river Tame. During the Middle Ages development was slow though the population increased. An old document, probably of the early fifteenth century, lists fifteen men: ' This tellyth who shall be balys yn Bylston ', that is, the customary tenants to collect the Lord of the Manor's chief rent.[7] With their families, servants, under-tenants and so forth, the population would be about 200 souls.

As early as the fourteenth century it is recorded that coal and ironstone were mined, being found close to the surface. Although the huge potential of the deposits was not yet realised, the origins of an industrial development, side by side with agriculture, are evident.[8]

For a long time Bilston was a constablewick attached to the Wolverhampton Manor of Stowheath, and the present Greyhound Inn in the High Street, the oldest building in the town, stands on the site of the old Manor or Court House.[9] The present Stowheath Lane used to mark part of the boundary between Bilston and Wolverhampton.

In 1458, during the reign of Henry VI, a chantry or chapel was founded by Sir Thomas, ' de Erdington ', an area now part of Birmingham, and dedicated to St. Leonard.[10] This was not the first church building in Bilston; a smaller place of worship had been in existence for a long time. By a deed dated 1378, members of the Robyns family gave land for the support of a priest of Bilston, Sir William Poort.[11] This family owned much land in the area and was prominent for several centuries up to the eighteenth century.

The new chapel was under the eccesiastical control of the

mother church at Wolverhampton and the priest could not conduct weddings or funerals in Bilston. About eleven years after de Erdington's gift of land and rents, we find the name of some Bilston men who also granted land to help support the priest and, as in the case of the Robyns family, their families continued in prosperity for a long time, for example, John Mollesley, Richard Tomkys, William Robins, William Kempson, William Pype and William Perry.[12] It is probable that some of these were engaged in the expanding wool trade.

By the time of the Tudor period Bilston was a pleasant village with a number of good houses of timber, plaster, thatch and leaded windows. In documents of that period it was spelt as both 'Bileston' and 'Billeston'.[13] The inhabitants were engaged in agricultural pursuits, but more men were using coal and iron to manufacture small items to meet local needs and learning the skills of working and fashioning metals. In addition to the coal and iron deposits, there was also the sand for casting described by Dr. Plot as follows: 'I met with a sort of sand at Bilston so very fine that it is hardly palpable. It is of a deep orange colour'.[14] Farm labourers and shepherds had craftsmen as neighbours; in 1540 we have a certain John Foxhall described as a locksmith. The Victoria History of Staffordshire refers to 'hammer men' in 1578 and 1585[15], and mentions a forge at Sedgley and a furnace at Ettingshall, two places adjoining Bilston, where, no doubt, similar work was being done.

It would be wrong to imagine Bilston, in Elizabethan times, as an isolated village, cut off from the main stream of English life and history. Though it consisted of a snake-like thoroughfare with houses and shops set in garden patches or bordering fields, yet it was on the main London to Holyhead road and even though travellers to and from the north and Ireland or London might rest briefly at Wolverhampton, nevertheless the inhabitants of Bilston were familiar with local and national events. This is seen, perhaps, in the case of the Pipe family; Sir Richard Pipe was sheriff of London in 1572 and served Queen Elizabeth as Lord Mayor of the city in 1578.[16] At the same time we find his name heading a list of the tithe rentals for the town, and his family coat-of-arms was in Bilston Chapel.[17] It is interesting to note that there is a building known by older

10

residents as the Pipe Hall and nearby is Pipe's Meadow. The locally known 'Orchard' was probably part of the family property. There is a tablet in the Carousel Inn near the Post Office in Hall Street commemorating Sir Richard Pipe, this hotel building being the old locally-known 'Pipe Hall'.

The population steadily increased during the Tudor and Stuart period. The chief rent about 1600 amounted to £5.4s.5½d.[18] from 23 occupiers and by 1700 the chief tenants had more than trebled in number. The Hearth Tax return for 1660 gives a population of 101 householders as yielding £10.2s.2d. and that of 1675 has 105.[19] A return for 1695 gives the population, including children, as 1002 with some 180 houses.[20]

By this time, in South Staffordshire, the manufacture of small articles in metal was developing. The Victoria History of Staffordshire states: 'By the early seventeenth century a picture emerges of a well-established iron industry in the county. The balance of production was becoming weighted towards the south'.[21] Henry Powle, writing about the iron trade in 1677, states that pig iron was being worked in Staffordshire forges and brought to local workshops where it was made into hardware goods. When the celebrated Dr. Plot[22] visited Bilston in the year 1686 he writes of a stone quarry and of the quality of the grinding stones produced. Of the coal output, he states that 12 or 14 collieries were producing a total of up to 5,000 tons a year. A document of 1690 dealing with Draft Deeds in the William Salt Library refers to five bore holes for coal being made in the Roger fields, four of which were successful. At a depth of 11 to 14 yards seams of coal at least seven feet thick were found.

The type of work carried out was to some degree localised and organised as a domestic industry; Wolverhampton and Willenhall made locks, nails were produced at Dudley and Sedgley, chains at Cradley. The Sedgley registers[23] and local wills have frequent references to 'home' craftsmen at this period, the chief being that of 'naylor' though several 'sythsmiths' are recorded. One interesting will is that of Richard Ellwall of Ettingshall, 'naylor', dated 20.7.1634. who left 'To my daughters Dorothie and Anne my old cowe called Gusle to be equally divided between them. To my three sons all my smithy, tools, stocks, bellies, etc.'; the latter were bellows. Richard Raybould, whose

11

will is dated 11.7.1672., was a 'sythsmith' who left an estate of over £500.

The small workshops were family units whose output, later on, was exploited by the men who supplied the iron, but, on occasion, neighbours probably combined interests as is seen in the case of Edward Oakley, 'lockier', in whose will proved 11.9.1721., there is the following: 'Item, one fifth part of a cole pitt and a fifth part of a house'.

The Rev. Richard Ames, who was curate at Bilston from 1684 till 1730, when recording births and deaths in the parish register, used to add the occupation of the father, and in the period 1716-1730 we find about 100 bucklemakers, over 50 chapemakers and, in addition, there are toymakers (making trinkets and 'trifles'), boxmakers, a few hingemakers, tinder-box makers, locksmiths and two japanners. In some instances one man may be described, in different entries, as engaged in more than one of the trades.

Of outstanding interest to us, when thinking about the enamelling trade to come, are the manufacturers of 'toys', boxes, hinges and buckles, for their products were the basic items on which the enamellers depended. The availability of cheap coal and iron has been mentioned, and in addition good quality sand and limestone was at hand. Copper was obtainable from the north-east of the county[24], the mines being at Ecton, Ribden, Calton Moor, Upper Elkstone, Mixon, Swinscoe and Waterfall. The Ecton mines were said to have been re-discovered in 1720 and much high grade ore was obtained. In fact between 1760 and 1768 copper worth nearly £57,000 was mined. The manufacture and use of alloys became increasingly developed in the South Staffordshire area and in Birmingham, while the Stourbridge area could provide excellent silica and fine glass. A Richard Cumberlidge was working as a brassfounder in Bilston in 1720[25]. Copper was the principal metal needed for enamelling as it was easy to shape, and finely-rolled copper sheets became available from South Wales.

Though these early eighteenth century Bilston craftsmen worked in their own homes or small backyard 'shops' or premises, they were sufficiently established and known to take apprentices as the following shows[26]:

12

MASTER	TRADE	APPRENTICE	DATE
Thomas Allen	Toymaker	John Ballard	23.12.1713.
		(Abbot's Morton)	
		Martin Ballard	10. 8.1715.
		(Northwick)	
Joseph Allen	,,	Francis Bailey	4. 9.1721.
John Mousell	,,	William Ebbral	14.11.1721.
Dovey Hawksford	,,	William Homer	2. 2.1722.
		(Walsall)	
		Thomas Steward	15. 9.1722.
		(Walsall)	
Joseph Buckley	,,	Samuel Chase	2.10.1729.
Samuel Ball	,,	John Persehouse	13.11.1729.
John Davies	Boxmaker	Amos Davies	8. 9.1730.

John Mousell was the son of Susanna, who later married John Bickley, and William Ebbral, the apprentice, was a witness to her will (16.3.1727.) where he signs as Eborall.

John Davies was the son of Edward Davies who died in 1751, described in his will as a boxmaker of Bilston, but the inventory of his goods only amounted to £1.15s.10d. An entry in Aris's Gazette, Birmingham, for 27.6.1748. stated that Catherine, wife of John Davies of Bilston, boxmaker, had eloped.

If we continue the list beyond 1730 we find the following employers:

Joseph Parker	Toymaker	12.10.1738.
Benjamin Bickley	,,	19. 2.1742.
John Bratt	,,	7.11.1742.
John Green	,,	24.10.1742.
Richard Ames (Nephew) ...	,,	10.11.1743.
William Arnold	,,	1. 8.1743.
Benjamin Bickley	,,	16.11.1743.
	,,	6. 8.1744.
	,,	6. 9.1744.
John Green	,,	30. 6.1744.
Samuel Stone	,,	4. 3.1744.

There are gaps in the records from 1731 until 1741, and from 1745 until 1750, but additional entries are:

William Arnold		14. 2.1749.
Isaac Beckett (Senior)		15. 4.1751.

Thomas Bayliss took Hannah Taylor as an apprentice 29.5.1755. He is described as a 'boxpainter' and the above list contains the names of some of the principal Bilston enamellers.

We get additional information from the List of Indentures as follows:

APPRENTICE	MASTER	TRADE	DATE	PERIOD
Thomas Mason	Sarah Mason	Bucklemaker	1706	7 years
John Shale	Thomas Allen	,,	1701	2½ years
Joseph Stephen	John Stephen	,,	1705	7 years
Robert Davies	Frank Taylor	,,	1706	2 years
William Allen	Thomas Beavon	,,	1718 till	24 years
John Mose	George Fenney	,,	1721 till	21 years
Joseph Wannorton	William Hickman	Toymaker	1723 till	24 years
Joseph Davies	Edward Lees	,,	1732 till	24 years
Noah Jenks	William Pearson	,,	1732 till	24 years
John Porter	,,	,,	1723 till	24 years
James Pool	Thomas Perry	,,	1725 till	24 years
William Pool	,,	,,	1725 till	24 years
William Blakemore	Walter Wood	Boxmaker	1725 till	24 years
William Martin	James Allsop	Toymaker	1726 till	24 years
James Fletcher	John Cooper	,,	1732 till	24 years

Again, if we continue the list, we find the local trades named over and over again till 1772, but if we confine ourselves to the approximate start of enamelling in Bilston, some time about 1750, we have these additional names:

BUCKLEMAKERS[27]
Charles Riley, William Barker, Thomas Shale, Henry Pearson, John Bate, Anthony Lees, George Hartill, Richard Hickman.

CHAPE MAKERS
Thomas Bate, Samuel Ashford, Thomas Mason, Richard Wilkes, Benjamin Povey, James Allen.

CHAPE FILERS
Thomas Sayton, William Tonks.

TOYMAKERS
James Compson, James Hartill, Alec Taylor, Joseph Baker, William Knowles, John Castey.

BOXMAKER
John Pinson.

In his book ' The Mode in Footwear ', R. Turner Wilcox[28], writing about the eighteenth century modes, states that the shoe buckles worn by men and women enjoyed a vogue of over a century. They were made of gold, silver, bronze and cut steel, engraved, enamelled and encrusted with diamonds, pearls, marcasite or paste jewels according to one's wealth. The Bilston products were of the less expensive varieties. With regard to the boxmakers we must distinguish between the strong, iron boxes for holding domestic valuables, such as deeds and cash, or jewellery, or church monies belonging to church wardens and

Overseers of the Poor, and the smaller, lighter boxes such as snuff boxes, patch boxes, and pill boxes.

In considering the above lists it must be remembered that these were men who could accommodate additional ' hands ' and that other craftsmen, not named, worked alone or with members of their family. Very often, too, they had interests in the land and livestock, raising crops, getting coal and minerals, felling timber and keeping the odd cow and a few pigs and fowls; some combined their trade with running an ale house. They were in humble circumstances, for the number of freeholders who voted at the general election of 1747 was merely nine in Bilston.

A point of interest is that girls' names occur in the lists, for instance Mary Moss went to Thomas Shale in 1730 to learn bucklemaking, as did Anne Mullabee to John Bate in 1746 and Mary Lees to Anthony Lees, perhaps father or uncle, in the same year. Francis Sayton, a chape filer, took Hannah Sutton in 1749. A noteworthy name is Hannah Taylor who joined Thomas Bayliss (29.5.1755.) to learn the art of boxpainting, that is most probably, enamelling.

Of course many other girls would be helping their fathers or brothers at home without being apprenticed. The apprentices either came from families who could afford the fees or they were placed by the Overseers of the Poor. They had a hard life with stern, exacting and sometimes cruel masters, so that it is not surprising to hear of individuals running away from intolerable conditions and their masters advertising their disappearance.

It is more than probable that some of the men named in this chapter became enamellers, apart from those we shall deal with in more detail later, or enamelling became an addition to their craft or that of their sons. A later chapter gives more facts about these men, for on their work and products depended the livelihood of the enamellers.

In conclusion, then, we see that there was a big production of buckles, boxes, trinkets, ' trifles ' and the like in the first half of the century; much of it went to centres such as Wolverhampton, Birmingham, and London for distribution[29]. How much more attractive and valuable these boxes, ' toys ' and buckles would be if beautified with all the lovely colours of enamel work.

15

REFERENCES

[1] Price, p. 20, quoting Shaw's 'Hist. of Staffordshire'.
[2] 'Staffordshire Domesday', by H. M. Fraser, p. 7. Also *S.R.S.*, 1919, p. 171.
[3] Lawley, p. 16. Inquisition, The Royal Domain of Wolverhampton, *S.R.S.*, 1911.
[4] Lawley, p. 17.
[5] Ibid.
[6] Lawley, p. 21.
[7] Parish Register, p. 164.
[8] 'Victoria Hist. of Staffordshire', Vol. 2, p. 72.
[9] 'S.R.S.', 1939, p. 229.
[10] Price, p. 22.
[11] Parish Register, p. 173.
[12] Price, p. 22.
[13] Price, p 15, and other variants in Parish Register, p. 164.
[14] Pitt, 'A Topographical Hist. of Staffordshire', p. 179.
[15] 'Victoria Hist. of Staffordshire', Vol. 2, p. 113.
[16] Lawley, p. 146, Parish Register, p. 169.
[17] Lawley, p. 36.
[18] Price, p. 31.
[19] 'S.R.S.', 1923, p. 62-64.
[20] Price, p. 52.
[21] Victoria Hist. of Staffordshire', Vol. 2, p. 113.
[22] Dr. Robert Plot, 'The Natural Hist. or Staffordshire', 1686. See 'Bilston'.
[23] Dudley Reference Library.
[24] 'Victoria Hist. of Staffordshire', Vol. 2, p. 266.
[25] Parish Register, p. 70.
[26] Transcripts of Apprenticeship Records, 1710-1745, (MSS) by Gerald Mander, Wolverhampton Ref. Library.
[27] Births in Parish Register from 1716 give occupation of father.
[28] p. 118.
[29] H. Read, Cross currents in English Porcelain Glass and Enamels, *T.E.C.C.*, 1930.

2

ENAMELLING IN ENGLAND
BEFORE THE 18th CENTURY

THE art of enamelling on metal was known from early times
and followed the discovery of making glass and staining it
with powders made from different oxides of metal. It was practised in China, India, Byzantium and other civilisations and was
not unknown to the Britons of the Roman occupation.

A beautiful example of early work is the King Alfred jewel,
a pear-shaped object nearly 2½ inches long, having on one side a
three-quarter length figure in green with a red girdle, and carrying a gold sceptre in each hand[1]. The reverse side is of gold
plate with a tree pattern engraved, the whole work being of a
high standard. There are other examples of the period, such as
brooches, and no doubt some monks produced work for religious
purposes.

Following the Norman Conquest, England had close ties
with France where the technique of enamelling was highly
developed. The use of brightly coloured enamel work for areas
too large for insetting a precious stone or pearl was the answer
for craftsmen working in gold and silver for royal, ecclesiastical or
other wealthy patrons. Two early centres were in the valleys of
the rivers Meuse and Rhine[2], and the later famed Limoges
enamellers became renowned throughout Europe[3] and remained
so for centuries, although the town was sacked by the Black
Prince in 1371.

One can imagine a few monks in some monastery engaged
in the related arts of illuminating manuscripts, binding books and
making objects for religious use turning to enamelling to em-
bellish their work. These men used precious metals and produced
exquisite examples of croziers, chalices, ciboria, altar pieces,
reliquaries, and plaques for the covers of the precious hand-

17

written books. Often enamelled pieces were combined with pearls and precious stones in the making of rich vestments and altar frontals. At the same time goldsmiths and silversmiths were using enamel to enhance their excellent work for kings, courtiers and other wealthy clients.

Monks took their technical knowledge to other religious foundations and taught the craft, while craftsmen moved to other royal courts or capital cities to improve their fortunes. The crozier of William of Wykeham, of about 1400 A.D. is the finest surviving piece of ecclesiastical metal work enriched with enamel[4].

So established had the art become that men were also writing about it. The Benedictine monk Theophilus wrote a treatise[5], which included an account of the process involved, about the year 1200, and Benvenuto Cellini (1500-1571) had, among his other exceptional talents, great skill as an enameller, as is seen, for instance, in his oustandingly beautiful gold and enamelled salt cellar[6]; he describes his methods in his 'Tratiato dell Oreficeria ': Enamelling is just the same as painting, he asserts.

In the Middle Ages there were two principal methods of applying enamel to a metal surface. The first was to mark off, in outline, the required design or pattern, then with a sharp tool small amounts of metal were removed to form shallow cavities. Into these enamel paste would be pressed to a depth of $\frac{1}{32}''$ to $\frac{1}{16}''$ approximately. The bottom of the recess would be scored to help secure the enamel. The paste was carefully applied with a spatula or small brush to remove any air bubbles. When completely dry the object was fired in a small furnace. At the right temperature fusion would take place and, after cooling, the process would be repeated until the hollows were filled and the surface of the enamel was very slightly above that of the metal. When cool the enamel was carefully ground to give a smooth surface with the metal. This method was known as ' champlevé '—raised field—and required most careful workmanship[7]. There are some splendid examples of this type of work in London museums, one being a fine reliquary casket in the British Museum, dated 1180-90. Here parts of the costumes are enamelled but the details of face, hands, and so on are left as incised lines on the metal.

Another method of applying the enamel was known as

18

'cloisonné' work from the French word 'cloison'[8]. After the design had been transferred to the metal surface very finely rolled gold wire was shaped to the guide lines and soldered into position. These formed 'boundary walls' between which the enamel paste was pressed. After firing and cooling, additional layers were added and procedure was then similar to that employed in champlevé work.

It is obvious that this method required great skill and patience, but some very fine work was done, particularly on gold and silver. In the age of chivalry, with the love of, and pride in, family coats of arms and the endless arrangements of design and colour required, there was great demand for enamelled work. Edward III (1327-1377) had an ewer enamelled with illustrations of the knights of the Round Table and his plate was enamelled with shields of arms. The royal accounts also refer to brooches in the design of his badges, and there are enamelled shields, in champlevé, on Edward's tomb in Westminster Abbey. On June 8th 1354 Edward gave four enamelled cups to some French visitors and in 1365 he bought from Thomas Hessey, a London goldsmith, 50 cups, ewers, saltcellars, all silver gilt and enamelled[9].

Up to the 11th century, enamelling was an adjunct to the work of the goldsmiths, an additional embellishment to their skills with metal, but later enamelling became an art form in its own right and an independent craft.

The use of the words 'champlevé and 'cloisonné' indicate the supremacy of the French enamellers at the time, and Limoges was pre-eminent. Chamot states that Limoges acquired the monopoly of 'champlevé' enamelling[10]. Yet another type of work done in the medieval period, on gold and silver, was known as 'bassetaille' and this came into favour in the fifteenth century at the expense of 'champlevé' which went out of fashion.

Here the picture or design was cut in low relief and a translucent enamel was applied to the whole surface. Variations in the depth of the incisions produced varying intensity of colour. This method was not so frequently used as the other two.

These techniques, however, could not be used for fine, detailed work, for instance the varied colourings on a person's face, but near the end of the 15th century, at Limoges, successful experiments were made in applying small amounts of enamel

19

paste with a fine brush. In 'Limoges Enamels' by W. and B. Forman, with text by M. Gauthier and M. Marcheix[11], it is asserted that the oldest painted enamels are two small medallions of about 1450 by Jean Fouquet and that after 1500, with the exception of work produced at Venice, Limoges possessed the complete monopoly of enamel painting on metal during the whole of the 16th century. This method was less laborious and involved, and meant that more interesting and varied work was possible. Given the metal worker's finished metal object there was now work for the artist—the painter in enamels. There are examples of large Limoges enamels painted in the 16th century such as those from the Courtoy workshop. These include dishes decorated on both sides and also portraits as large as twelve inches by fifteen inches. The predominant colour is a rich blue but a red, green, brown, yellow, violet and black were gradually made available. The Limoges enamellers also discovered the value of applying a coat of enamel on the reverse side of the plate to prevent warping during successive firings; this is called 'counter-enamelling'.

The method of painting the enamel colours on to the metal was used in England and throughout Europe till the advent of transfer printing about the middle of the eighteenth century, but even then fine individaul pieces continued to be produced. This technique led to some artists experimenting with the idea of portrait miniatures. Such portraits done in paint on vellum, or later on in ivory, had proved to be highly popular with the wealthy and prosperous and royal appointments were made of such painters of miniatures to the Court as Isaac Oliver[12].

Two famous miniature painters of the early Stuart period were Samuel Cooper (1609-1672) and John Hoskins; their pieces are highly valued today.

Dr. George C. Williamson in his book 'Portrait Miniatures'[13] states that Jean Petitot (1607-1671) stands out supreme as a miniature painter in enamel, having mastered the craft in France. He had worked at the court of Louis XIV and had been influenced by the work of Van Dyck. There are fine examples of his work in Windsor Castle and the South Kensington Museum.

There were other foreigners who set up in business in England, especially in London. Such was Michael Dahl from Sweden in 1687 who started a school in London and was appointed Court Enameller to William III and Mary in 1696. Dr. Williamson writes: 'When it is remembered that the colours were painted on to a panel of gold in the form of a powder, only slightly mingled with a medium, that they did not represent by their tint the colour they were to represent when fused and the slightest error in fusing would ruin the plate and cause the colours to run into one another, the marvel is but enhanced when the exquisite works produced by these incomparable artists are examined '.

Other noteworthy miniature painters of the later part of the seventeenth century were Thomas Flatman, Richard Gibson and Nicholas Dixon, and the great popularity of the work of these artists is seen in the story of the Blenheim Enamel.

Charles Boit was commissioned to execute a piece[14] of enamel work 24″ x 16″ from a design by Laguerre to commemorate Marlborough's famous victory at Blenheim in 1704. In the design the Duke is being led to Queen Anne by 'Victory'. The queen's husband advanced £1,000 for a special furnace to be built and to meet other costs, but technical difficulties arose and, although a further £1,000 was advanced by the Treasury, the work was never completed, and interest in the project declined when Anne quarrelled with the Duke's wife.

In the end Boit fled to France, but the story illustrates the technical knowledge and skill he and his assistants must have possessed to tackle such an ambitious piece of work.

G. Reynolds in his book 'English Portrait Miniatures'[15] states 'Boit's enamels, technically, are excellent. Because of his mastery of the craft he implanted the admiration for enamel painting in the taste of English patrons, a taste which, during the half century it lasted, helped to depress the national school of painting in water colours '.

Another foreign enameller, Zincke, who was born in Dresden[16] in 1683, came to England to assist Boit with the Blenheim Enamel but he set up his own establishment and later received commissions from George II and members of the royal family. This set the seal on his popularity and, painting from the life, he was able to charge between 20 and 30 guineas; he became so busy that he had to employ assistants and apprentices who probably did 'filling-in' work. These successful miniature painters would have a muffle furnace on their premises and either carried out personally the firings or else supervised them.

The success of the miniaturists led to the formation of a group of artists who specialised in the production of tiny oval paintings of about $1\frac{1}{2}''$ in diameter instead of the usual $3\frac{1}{2}''$; two well known masters in this delicate work were Gervase Spencer and Nathanial Hone.

The enthusiasm for all kinds of works of art from the Continent—particularly France—led to much imitation in England and this included attempts to copy enamelled boxes and trinkets. A few men in London would appear to have attempted this in about the 1740s[17]. Another example of this imitation is the production of enamelled watch cases. The British Museum has examples including one containing a watch by the celebrated Thomas Tompion of about 1690, enamelled by a Frenchman. The enamelling might take the form of a coloured design or a portrait.

The story of the painters of miniatures does not end here, at about the half-way stage in the eighteenth century, but the purpose of this outline is to show that the art and technique of enamelling was well known and established in England before it became an important trade in Bilston in the second half of that same century.

REFERENCES
1 M. Chamot, ' Medieval Enamels ', p. 2 (and Plate 1a).
2 M. Chamot, op. cit., p. 8. ' Oxford Hist. of English Arts ', ii, 194. ' Encyclopæ of World Art ', iv, 735 and 741.
3 Ibid., p. 743.
4 M. Chamot, op. cit., p. 16, and Plate 20c.
5 ' Encyclopædia of World Art ', Vol. iv, p. 735.
6 H. Cunnyngham, ' European Enamels ', pp. 62-65.
7 Ibid., pp. 90-100.
8 Ibid., pp. 62-65.
9 ' Oxford Hist. of English Arts ', iv, 62.
10 H. Chamot, op. cit., p. 11.
11 p. 10.
12 Bryan's ' Dictionary of Painters and Engravers ', pp. 36-37.
13 pp. 71-73. G. Reynolds, ' English Portrait Miniatures ', pp. 68-69.
14 H. Cunynghame, op. cit., pp. 146-148. G. Reynolds, ' English Portrait Miniatures ', p. 98.
15 pp. 96-100.
16 Ibid., pp. 112-116.
17 A. J. Toppin, ' Notes on Jansen and Artists at Battersea Factory ' T.E.C.C., 1932.

3

THE ENAMELLING PROCESS

IT would be convenient to establish what is meant by enamel. The Concise Oxford Dictionary defines it as 'a glass-like opaque or semi-transparent coating of metallic surfaces for ornament or as a preservative lining'. It is the result of the fusion, under heat, of a paste of which the basic ingredients are soda, potassium silicates, lead oxide and silica. In short, enamel is a kind of stained glass applied as a paste to the surface of some object made of metal such as gold or silver, if very choice and valuable, but more frequently copper, though it can be successfully applied to most other metals and alloys.

The enamel may be opaque, usual, or transculent and the various colours and tints are the result of adding various metallic[1] oxides, reduced to very fine powder, in certain proportions. Generally speaking, the more oxide used the darker the colour.

Let us suppose that the object to be enamelled is a snuff box. A 'toymaker' or boxmaker will have made and shaped the box and its separate hinged lid out of copper or copper alloy. By the middle of the eighteenth century, good quality copper, capable of being rolled into thin sheets pressed into various shapes, was available from South Wales. Another advantage was that it could withstand high temperatures. In addition, at places like Birmingham, new forms of metal were being successfully produced.

We will now confine our attention to the lid of the box. This must be carefully and thoroughly cleaned and dried ready for the application of the enamel. In the early days long hours had to be spent preparing the powders from which the different coloured effects would be obtained. With pestle and mortar, and in distilled water, the various metallic oxides, silica and fine glass would be separately ground down, sifted and ground again, often by children, till the resulting powder could be strained and allowed to dry thoroughly.

The first coating applied would be a mixture of silica, oxide of lead, potash and soda, made into a paste. This would be applied to one side of the lid, any surplus removed and then left to dry out. The lid was ready for firing now. It was placed in a 'muffle' furnace, so called because the draught created was 'muffled' or damped down to reduce the oxidation. If it is remembered that the fuel was coal, that there were no such things as thermostats or controls as on modern electric kilns, that the enameller depended on his eye and experience for the 'rightness' of firing conditions and temperatures, then one begins to appreciate the skill required to obtain successful results after several repeated firings of the same piece.

The furnace would be an iron box with a door to open at the front. Smoke and fumes from the burning coal would thus be excluded. The objects to be fired would be placed in a fireclay container and carefully placed in the furnace. When cheaper transfer work was being done the container might have a double layer of small items all to be fired simultaneously.

After cooling, the lid was taken out and a coating of white or creamy-white enamel paste was applied. The process might then be repeated till the required thickness of the enamel layer was obtained. In a similar manner the underside of the lid would be treated. Later on a thick creamy paste of white enamel could be applied to both sides, but allowed to dry separately, and fired simultaneously. The application of the enamel pastes on top of the basic ground coat and their fusion was not difficult, providing their melting points were lower than that of the ground coat; this also helped in the avoidance of 'running' of the colour.

The application of a thick coat of enamel on both sides of thin copper was the best answer to the problem of expansion and contraction during and after the firings, a slightly convex surface was also a help in avoiding cracking.

The edges of the lids, plaques, and such items were sometimes difficult to enamel satisfactorily so gilt or copper frames were used, or the piece of work could be inserted into a frame or inset into a lid; a gold box, for instance, might have an

24

enamelled picture on the lid.

The decoration could now begin, assuming that both parts of the box had now the necessary primary coats applied on both sides. A typical treatment was to put a picture or scene on the lid and simpler decoration on the sides and perhaps on the inside too. If a fine piece of work is planned then a 'boxpainter' with artistic ability is essential for the lid decoration at least, though assistants or apprentices might be entrusted to decorate the sides with, for example, simple floral designs or patterns, or even a single colour all over.

The knowledge of what ingredients to use, and in what proportions, came as a result of trial and error, not from textbooks, and it is probable that the master kept to himself the secrets of how he achieved tints and effects. It is interesting to read what a writer in the early fourteenth century had to say about the preparation of enamel[2]. He writes: 'Enamel is thus made. Take lead and melt it, continually taking off the pellice which floats on the surface until the whole lead is wasted away; of which take one part and of the powder here-after mentioned as much; and this is the said powder. Take small white pebbles which are found in streams and pound them into most subtle powder; and if you wish to have yellow enamel add oil of filberts and stir with a hazel rod; for red add filings of latten, a kind of yellow alloy somewhat like brass, with calomine; for blue good azure lapis or saffre of which glaziers make blue glass'. As there is no mention of oxide of tin the enamel resulting would not be opaque but translucent.

The colours resulting from firing bore little resemblance to those applied beforehand and, here again, knowledge was acquired through experience. No doubt the master would build up a notebook of recordings of successful experiments for future use.

T. W. Hackwood, writing of enamellers in the neighbouring town of Wednesbury, states that best fine glass was important so broken goblets and glasses were collected from hotels and inns for powdering down[3]; the use of glass was in order to form the hard crystal-like foundation. Added were fine seasand, red lead, arsenic, gum arabic and other ingredients.

It has already been mentioned that some metallic oxides will produce certain colour effects without giving an opaque body

25

colour. The latter may be obtained from using tin or antimony as an additional ingredient.

In their book 'Enamelling' Lewis and Day[4] assert that different colours may be obtained from the same metal according to the nature of the oxide, the character of the glass and the heat to which it is subjected. From copper one may obtain ruby red, emerald green, turquoise blue, with a soda base. Coral red, sea green and brownish yellow came from iron, while cobalt provided most of the blues except turquoise. Manganese was needed to get purple; silver would give a clear yellow. These, with tin and antimony to provide white, made up practically the whole basic colour range of the enameller working in the period 1750-1800. Black was not used a great deal but it was obtained from a mixture of colours.

If the proportions of the ingredients were changed only a little, different tints resulted; these might arise from the presence of slight impurities or the conditions in the furnace; moreover the amount of the colouring oxide affected the light or dark shade of the fired enamel.

As the melting points of metals vary, it was necessary to fire first of all, the enamel requiring the highest temperature for fusion and, then, after cooling and re-application of enamel, progressively down the scale. It will be seen that several firings might be required to complete a picture or design and there was a number of occasions when something might go wrong and ruin the work so painstakingly done. In such a case it was, of course, possible to recover the metal base by plunging the piece directly from the furnace into cold water which caused the enamel to crack and dis-integrate. For repeated firings gold was the best metal to use to avoid tarnishing or discolouration.

Attempts have been made to date the first appearance of particular colours, dark blue at Chelsea in 1755, pale green 1759 and claret in 1760. We are on more reliable ground with 'Rose Pompadour', for about the year 1755 Madame de Pompadour, the renowned mistress of Louis XIV, and a great patron of the arts, had the china factory at Vincennes transferred to Sèvres nearer Paris[5]. She supervised operations and great artists went to work for her and were well paid. The beautiful pink known as 'Rose Pompadour' was first produced here and named in her honour; another discovery was apple green.

Boxpainters could, by this time, buy enamel powders from suppliers as the following advertisements in Aris' Gazette of Birmingham indicates:—[6]

2nd September 1751 and 16th September 1751

'Abraham Seaman, enamelling painter of Freeman Street, Birmingham, makes and sells all sorts of enamelling colours.

N.B.—Most of the eminent enamel painters of Birmingham, Wednesbury and Bilston have made use of the above colours to their satisfaction'. References will be made later to the significance of this date.

In the same paper, in October the following year, there is a notice from Mrs. Seaman, widow of Abraham, to inform the public that 'she continues to furnish the Rose-colour and best Red made fit for enamel and china painters in the same manner as in the life time of her husband, Abraham Seaman deceased, at Thomas Benton's, High Street, Birmingham'. The same Benton advertises on 2nd April 1753, a change of address but 'all enamel and china painters may be furnished as usual'. Mrs. Seaman, in an entry for 25th March 1754, lets the trade know that she has moved to Mr. Samuel Salts', corner of Church Street, 'where she will continue to sell the best red or rose-colour as usual'. It would appear that these two colours were a speciality of her husband, probably the outcome of much experimenting.

Another retailer, John Bennet, in Colemer's Row, advertises in 1756 that he also 'makes and sells the best Rose Red'.

While on the subject of colours, we must note the appearance in 1758 of the edition of 'The Handmaid to the Arts' by Robert Dossie. One chapter deals with enamelling and there is a list of thirty nine colours and their composition. Basically, they are various shades of red, pink, blue, yellow, green, orange, purple, brown and black. Azure blue does not appear before about 1760, but then it became very popular.

So far, in this chapter, we have been concerned with the enameller applying his colours with a brush, based on some picture, pattern or design of his own choice and his own artistic ability, each piece of work being unique and almost impossible to repeat exactly similar in every detail. We are, however, on the brink of a new discovery, one which was to revolutionise the

27

manufacture of enamelled goods, and articles of porcelain and japanned ware, that is the art of transfer printing.

The name of the man who first experimented successfully with this technique is disputed and various claims have been made. John Brooks, the Irishman, is discussed later on and his pioneer work in Birmingham in the early 1750s may probably entitle him to the distinction of being first in the field.

Another early experimenter was John Sadler of Liverpool, who demonstrated his new printing process in 1756[7]. The first attempts appear to have been in printing on tiles, where the prospects for a large output were encouraging.

Hackwood, the Wednesbury historian, claims to have had details of the process from a very old man who had been employed in a Wednesbury enamelling business,[8] and the various steps were as follows; the first requisite was a metal block on which the engraver could incise all the lines to make his picture or design. This is very skilful and patient work, for one slip of the engraving tool might ruin work on which much time had been spent.

Suitable ink or printing black which would stand the test of firing, when it became burnt into the enamel, was prepared. In addition to black, shades of red, brown or purple were sometimes used. The ink was spread over the engraved plate with a piece of beaver, care being taken to fill in all the lines. The surplus ink was then wiped off and the inked lines checked, particularly those only lightly incised

A piece of gummed paper was now applied by means of a pair of wooden rollers so that the complete design was transferred to the paper. The imprinted paper now had to be carefully, separated and if any lines were not satisfactorily clear, especially in a portrait, scene, or calendar they could be ' touched up ' later. The paper, while still adhering to the plate, could, however, be placed in a drying store so that the ink would swell up and then dry on the paper.

The imprinted design or picture now had to be transferred to the box-lid or plaque which had already received its primary white enamel foundation. The paper was wetted and carefully placed in position. Firing in a muffle furnace now took place and at the correct temperature the design was burnt into the enamel and became fixed; the paper meanwhile burnt away.

A translucent glaze was then put over the whole surface and, after firing, the object might have no further treatment, as in the case of cheap little boxes; on the other hand it could be passed to the boxpainter for colouring.

The engraved plate, after cleaning, was ready for a repetition of the process on a second object and others in succession, in a form of mass production. The colour of the ink might be changed and another batch of transfers made. It is obvious, therefore, how important was the role of the engraver to the enameller. Having now considered how enamelling was done we must turn to the origin and development of the trade in Bilston.

REFERENCES
[1] Henley's 'Twentieth Century Formulas', p. 293. Edited by G. D. Hiscox.
[2] 'Archeological Journal', Vol. 2, 1876, p. 172. Partly quoted by M. Chamot, op. cit., p. 14.
[3] 'Wednesbury Workshops', p. 15.
[4] p. 194.
[5] B. Rackham, 'Porcelain as a Sidelight on Battersea Enamels', *T.E.C.C.*, 1932.
[6] Birm. R. L.
[7] W. Turner, 'Transfer Printing on Enamels, Porcelain and Pottery' Chapter 1.
[8] F. W. Hackwood, 'Wednesbury Workshops', pp. 13-17.

4

ENAMELLING IN BILSTON

THE types of work done in Bilston in the early decades of the 18th century — buckles, 'toys' and boxes — indicate the natural development towards attempts to beautify the products with enamel. Who began enamelling in the town, it is difficult to decide.

It has been suggested that perhaps a refugee from the Huguenot religious persecution in France who had been engaged in the trade settled in Bilston[1]. We know that many such people came to England and that skilled enamellers from the continent had frequently come across the Channel. If such a Protestant craftsman came one might expect to find some record in the parish registers but there is nothing conclusive.

It has been pointed out that there was a continuous history of enamelling in England with London the chief centre, and that official court appointments were made of enamellers. Moreover if, in Elizabeth's reign, a son of the Pipe family named Richard could succeed in business so well as to be made Sheriff of London in 1572 and Lord Mayor in 1578, it is not beyond the bounds of possibility that a young man in the 18th century might have been sent from Bilston to be apprenticed to an enameller, learn the trade and return to set up a workshop. After all the work of the bucklemakers, toymakers and boxmakers would be greatly enhanced and made marketable by the addition of enamel; it would be feasible that some such craftsman paid for his son to be apprenticed to an enameller elsewhere and then engaged him in similar work at home.

Another possibility is that someone began experimenting with a little knowledge gained outside Bilston; it must be remembered that the japanning trade was also established in the town in the first half of the 18th century[2]. Among the variety of objects produced were japanned snuff boxes and there are examples of such boxes with inset enamelled lids. Hutton in his 'History of Birmingham' suggests that the enamelling of boxes developed from this.

Whatever the origins, enamelling was being carried on in Bilston before 1750 as the Seaman advertisements would appear to indicate,[3] and it is quite certain that it was not as a consequence of the closing of the Battersea factory in 1756. This famous enamelling business had been started in London at York House by Theodore Jansen, a successful merchant and friend of artists, who became Lord Mayor of London in 1754. The factory is first mentioned in the Rate Book of 1753[4] but some have stated the work started about 1750. The Rate Book shows Jansen, Delamain and Brooks as proprietors for the third quarter of 1753, Messrs. Jansen and Company for the same quarter of 1754, and for the last quarter of 1756 indicates that the place was unoccupied.

Jansen had a first-class team of artists in his employ including Simon-Francois Ravenet, a French artist and engraver[5], the young Robert Hancock, another engraver, Henry Delamain, a potter who had specialised in tile decoration, and John Brooks, a Dublin engraver. Brooks has been credited with the introduction of transfer printing and he probably began his first experiments in Birmingham before moving to Battersea.[6]

In his work on transfer printing, William Turner notes that Ravenet was born in Paris in 1706 and died in London 1774, and that he introduced stronger, or deeper, etching in ground laying. He was in London some five years before Battersea opened, and during that time he worked, amongst others, for Hogarth in producing prints of his paintings; he also did portrait plates of George I and George II, the poets Pope, Thompson and others.

Egan Mew, writing about Battersea enamels in 1926 states 'the honour and glory . . . in the matter of transfer printing belong to Ravenet and Battersea'.[7]

W. B. Honey in his 'Foreword' to Cyril Cook's 'The Life and Work of Robert Hancock' asserts that John Brooks, Irish mezzotint engraver, was part-proprietor of the Battersea works. This would suggest that it was his mastery of the technique of transfer printing which was so valuable to Jansen.

Another man employed at Battersea was James Gwin who was in London about 1753. A. Pasquin in his 'The Authentic History of Painting in Ireland '[8] says that Gwin found employment as a designer for lids of snuff boxes at the Battersea Enamel Works. Cyril Cook in an article in ' Apollo ' 1952 states that at Battersea he designed religious, classical and allegorical subjects which Ravenet exquisitely engraved. He refers to one particular piece of work symbolising Britannia which has a contempory inscription on the back as follows: ' Drawn by Gwin, engraved by Ravenet for ye Battersea Manuf're under Sr. J. Theodore Jansen '.

Sayer's 'Artists' Vade Mecum ', 1776 edition, has some ' groups designed by Gwin and engraved by Mr. Ravenet '. He apparently did some engraving also but according to Cook, he was the chief designer at York House.

The work produced was of high artistic merit and beautifully executed, both tasteful and elegant and much appreciated by the high society of London. The outstanding feature was the quality of the engraving transfer printed on to the base of white enamel —the fine composition and beauty of line. With regard to colours, a warm, reddish brown was frequently used to enhance the outline and a bright crimson and clear blue were favoured. It is very probable that some of the articles made by Bilston and Birmingham toymakers, such as small boxes, went to Battersea for transfer printing and enamelling which was the prime purpose for setting up the business. Nevertheless, in a document[9] in which Jansen took on an apprentice, he is described as a ' toyman '.

Shortly afterwards he became bankrupt and the Daily Advertiser[10] of 28th February 1756 carried a notice of the sale of the factory which referred, in addition to enamel powders, to patterns and engraved plates ' snuff boxes of all sizes of great variety of Patterns of square and oval pictures of the Royal Family, History and other pleasing subjects, very proper ornaments for Cabinets of the Curious, Bottle tickets, with chains for all sorts of liquor, and of different subjects, Watch-cases, Toothpick-cases, Coat and Sleeve buttons, Crosses and other curiosities, mostly mounted, in metal, double gilt '.

In June of the same year the furniture, stock-in-trade, goodwill, and so forth were advertised and included were ' all the utensils etc. belonging to the manufactory, also a great number of copper plates, beautifully engraved by the best hands '.

A. J. Toppin in a paper on ' Notes on Jansen and the Artists[11] of the Battersea Factory ' gives the cause of the failure of the business as Brooks' bad habits and neglect of business.

He himself was declared bankrupt in 1756 and, after the closure of the factory, he earned a living by designing and engraving for booksellers and tried to get subscriptions for work ' in the enamelling process of which he kept the secret '. But his manner of life did not inspire confidence. He may not have stayed at York House for very long but some of his known work includes portraits of the Gunning sisters, Irish actresses and Horace Walpole.

The toymakers and boxpainters in Bilston must have been greatly interested in these sales, first because the ' best hands ' were now out of work and secondly because the equipment, including the valuable engraved plates, was available. It is quite possible that enamelling in the town improved in quality and certainly in output, particularly with regard to transfer printing of ' trifles ', box lids and the like. With regard to individuals Robert Hancock moved into the Midlands and his possible connection with Bilston is discussed later.

The first man to have attempted enamelling in Bilston was probably Dovey Hawksford. His family were no strangers to the town having resided there for some time, and were to continue doing so after his death. He was the son of Richard and Catharine Hawksford and was born in 1695; in the baptismal entry the curate, Ames, calls him ' my godson '.[12] His grandfather John Hawksford had been a locksmith and a benefactor to the church poor. Ames lived with John and his family when he went to Bilston. The Doveys included, at that time, Roger and Esther who had a son Richard born in 1698; he became an innkeeper. Dovey married Mary Smith in 1722. The entry is specially inserted in the Baptism Register as follows ' 16th May, 1722. Dovey Hawksford (my Godson) son of Richard Hawksford of Bilston, yeoman, and Mary Smith, daughter of Thomas Smith senior, of Bilston, yeoman, were married by me '. Mary died of a stroke and miscarriage in the following year. Dovey later remarried and of his children Richard survived him. The house was a double-fronted building opposite the site of the old Wesleyan Chapel.[13]

The Hawksfords were prominent in town and church affairs. Richard Hawksford in 1720 charged three acres of freehold land at Wednesfield to give ten shillings at Christmas to be shared by twenty poor people of St. Leonard's Church.[14] He was Dovey's father and about 1733 his aunt, Mrs. Sarah Hawksford, gave a silver paten for use at the communion service, possibly when the church extension was built. She was a lady of some means as her will shows; she died in 1745 but her connections with the toymakers and enamellers in the town are significant.

Dovey Hawksford was Chapel Warden in 1731, 1732 and 1741; he also served as Constable in 1738.[15] There is a page in the Vestry Book devoted to his disbursements as Constable, the whole amounting to £13. 14s. 0½d. When the pew seats in the new church were being sold we find him paying his guineas for seats for the family[16] and his name frequently occurs on parish documents as on 17th September 1733, when an Act of Parliament was passed for the repair of the road between the Bridge and Shift End. Two days labour had to be given and we find his name heading the list of commissioners and trustees. A little later we note that he ' perused and allowed ' the accounts of the Overseers of the Poor. Another interesting item refers to the building of a workhouse. It appears that Mrs. Sarah Pipe, in her will, left £40 to the parish, half of which went on road improvements and half towards the building of the workhouse. There is an entry for 4th November 1737 as follows ' Memorandum. Dovey Hawksford is to pay into the hands of William Hollis £20 towards building of the workhouse '. Perhaps Hawksford, with his many activities, had overlooked the matter or the work had been completed and payment was due. He devoted a great deal of his time to local affairs as has been indicated, and in 1744 he and Benjamin Bickley, discussed later, presented the accounts of the Overseers; 72 levies on property owners realised £201. 18s. 0d.

He might well have been a toymaker who subsequently added box-painting and enamelling to his business interests.[17] In the Register of Apprentices there is an entry which states that on 2nd February 1722 William, son of Thomas Homer of Walsall was apprenticed to Dovey Hawksford ' toymaker ' and in September of the same year he took Thomas, son of Charles Steward, of Walsall. Since William Homer became an enameller, and is so-called in 1745, it is reasonable to assume that he had done such work in Hawksford's workshop.[18]

Mr. Eric Benton, in a paper read to the Ceramic Circle (14th December 1968) has some interesting facts about Hawksford's visits to, and connections with, an enamel painter at Warwick named Thomas Paris. Here he would see work in progress and no doubt he asked many technical questions.

Dovey Hawksford died in 1749[19] and the Rev. Edward Best made this entry in his register, the 31st March 1749: 'Dovey Hawksford died in the prime of his age—much lamented by his acquaintances and dependents which were very numerous for he carried on a very extensive Trade to the Credit and Advantage of this part of the country'. He was certainly a pioneer and must have had great influence on those ' acquaintances and dependents ' who had similar interests. These will be discussed later.

The Christian name Dovey seems to have been popular in the family, occurring into the next century. One of his sons had been christened Dovey but he did not survive him, and another son, Richard gave the same name to one of his sons who also died young. An exception to the tragedy of early deaths was Dovey's mother Catharine, who lived to the age of about 66 years. His grandsons—John and Dovey—were concerned in the business of lockmaking and the manufacture of screws.

It is clear that by the year 1760 enamelling was being successfully practised in a number of workshops, both of individual pieces and transfer-prints, that japanning was done equally well, that other workshops provided the necessary copper objects while other craftsmen specialised in supplying mounts or hinges for boxes and other items.[20] The mounts were needed to set off such things as boxlids, portrait miniatures and plaques—and Benjamin Beckett (1753-1799) was one man engaged in the work; he must have supplied mounts to the more famous Beckett enamellers. Hackwood says that some of the Wednesbury enamellers bought mounts from Bilston manufacturers.[21]

Following this general survey we now pass to a more detailed account of the men engaged in the enamelling trade in Bilston which was at its peak in the approximate period 1760-1790.

REFERENCES

[1] G. B. and T. Hughes, 'English Painted Enamels', p. 87.
[2] W. H. Jones, 'Story of the Japan and Tinplate Working in Wolverhampton'.
[3] See above p. 27.
[4] Bernard Rackham in *T.E.C.C.*, iv, 1932. Two papers.
[5] Ibid.
[6] W. Turner, op. cit., pp. 21-24. Cyril Cook, 'Apollo' Mag., May 1952.
[7] 'Battersea Enamels', p. 1.
[8] Cyril Cook, 'Apollo' Mag., March 1952, pp. 66-69. 'His Ravenet and his engravings on Battersea Enamels', *T.E.C.C.*, quotes from Pasquin.
[9] H. Read, 'Cross Currents in English Porcelain, Glass and Enamels', *T.E.C.C.*, 1930.
[10] B. Rackham, 'Supplementary Notes on the Battersea Factory', *T.E.C.C.*, 1932.
[11] W. Chaffers, 'Marks and Monograms on Pottery and Porcelain', 3rd edition, p. 976. *T.E.C.C.*, iv, 1932.
[12] Parish Register, p. 13. B. and T. Hughes, 'English Painted Enamels', p. 87.
[13] Lawley, but see Price, p. 60.
[14] Price, p. 64.
[15] Vestry Book.
[16] Price, p. 43.
[17] K. Foster, 'Scent Bottles', p. 51.
[18] Bernard Hughes, 'Battersea and South Staffordshire Enamels', in 'Collecting Antiques', p. 25.
[19] Aris' Gazette described him as an enameller.
[20] G. B. Hughes, 'English Snuff Boxes', pp. 73-74.
[21] F. W. Hackwood, 'Wednesbury Ancient and Modern', p. 128.

5

THE BECKETT FAMILY

THE Beckett family was engaged in the enamelling trade for longer than any other in Bilston and there is still a street in the town known as Beckett Street; it was near one end of this street that the family owned or rented land.

The parish register from 1715 to 1730 lists a John and William Beckett who were cousins. William was the son of John Beckett, a vice maker, who died in 1717.[1] There is another John described in his will as a toymaker who left everything to his son William; his personal estate amounted to £14. 2s. 6d. This was made up as follows:—

'Wearing apparell and Money in Pockett'			...		£1.15s.0d.
Furniture in the Kitchen	...	...	...	...	£1.10s.0d.
Furniture in the Buttery	...	...	...	...	5s.0d.
Furniture in the First Room	...	...	...	...	£2. 4s.0d.
Furniture in the Second Room	...	...	...	...	£1. 0s.0d.
Shop Tooles	...	...	...	...	£1. 1s.6d.
One Cow	...	...	...	...	£5. 7s.0d.
Hay in the barn	...	...	...	...	10s.0d.
Muck	...	...	...	...	4s.0d.
Things out of sight	...	...	...	...	6s.0d.
					£14. 2s.6d.

He paid 2s.6d., in 1727, for the insertion in the Town Book of the consecration of St. Leonard's church burial ground. He died in 1730 and is described as a bucklemaker in the Burials Register, which also has an entry two months earlier of 'Elizabeth Beckett, wife of John Beckett, boxmaker'.

Another interesting early entry in the parish register is as follows:— 'Register of children not baptized according to the rites and ceremonies of the Church of England. 5th April 1699, Isaac, son of William Beckett. His father paid the duty which is 2s.'; he was a nailor. Also in May 1715 an Isaac, son of William Beckett junior, was baptized. This William was a buckle-maker. It would appear that it was the other William's son, Isaac, who was first concerned with the enamel trade, although he is described as a toymaker in 1751 when he took John, the son of John Wood, as an apprentice. He is also described as a toymaker in a document surrendering land to his use in January 1751. Isaac Beckett was Chapel Warden 1749-52. As this was an annual appointment it speaks well of his standing. He married Hannah Proud in 1737 and she bore him a succession of children of whom the sons, Isaac, Benjamin and Edward are the most important. He died in 1789 having been a widower for about two years.

The burial register for January 1787 has, in addition to Hannah, wife of Isaac Beckett, Anne, wife of Isaac Beckett, from which it would appear that father and son became widowers in the same month.

Benjamin has already been mentioned as a mount-turner, that is he excelled in producing the thin strips of metal which were put on the exposed edges of the enamelled copper to hide any metal showing, because it was difficult to coat the edges adequately. The mounts could be gilded, and patterns and designs might be incorporated as for the surround of an oval plaque. Bilston-made mounts were used in other centres.[2] Benjamin died in 1799, his estate being valued at less than £300. His wife Elizabeth and his brother Issac are named as executors and two sons, Edward (the eldest) and Benjamin (the youngest) are mentioned in his will.

Isaac the younger became an enameller and is so described in his brother's will, and also in a list of jurors for 1783. He was born in 1749 and lived to the great age of 86, being buried at Bilston on 8th March 1836; his life, in fact, covers practically the whole period of enamelling in the town. An old deed refers to the sale of 'land and premises in Roger Field' by Joseph Pagett to Isaac Beckett in which Pagett is described as a box-maker and Beckett as an enameller.[3] An interesting feature is that the transfer was 'at a rent of one Peppercorn, payable if demanded '. It may be that two men were in some form of partnership or co-operating closely in business.

Benjamin's eldest son Edward (1757-1803) was a japanner and it is quite possible that, on occasions, the two family concerns made use of the same painters and engravers. In his will dated 1802 he left instructions for his executors, one of whom was his brother Isaac, to sell the stock, tools and implements, goods and personal estate at their discretion and to carry on the trade of a japanner until such sale.

He was able to leave over £1,000 to his wife and children, among whom we find yet another Isaac, his eldest son. No doubt some of the tools and other equipment stayed in the Beckett family, for he left his house, shop, garden and so forth to his second son Joseph who was not yet 21 years old; but the amount of money left—judged by values of the day—indicates a prosperous business. His wife, Jane, survived him until 1826 and in the notice of her death in the Wolverhampton Chronicle[4] she is described as 'relict of Mr. Edward Beckett, japanner of Bilston'. The references to the Becketts in the lists of Apprentices and Indentures are surprisingly limited to the following:—

John Wood to Isaac Beckett 1751
Mary Bates to Isaac Beckett 1761

However the records are not complete and the probable employment of young members of the various branches of the family with the addition of local 'hands' provided an adequate labour force.

The trade directories published from time to time regularly have one or more Becketts listed under Bilston entries:—
The Birmingham Directory (Pearson and Rollason) 1781 on Page XXIV under 'Toys' 'It is not possible to particularize the various kind of toys made here—those sent to Germany, Amercia, and in short to every quarter of the globe'. The directory has an entry:—
Isaac Beckett — enamelled boxmaker. Also there is a Henry Beckett who made metal buttons which could, of course, be enamelled if required, as was commonly done in Birmingham. He was probably the Henry Beckett who married Margaret Ball in 1754 and later her widowed sister in 1759, Margaret dying in 1756. Their son Henry, born in 1764, was the only surviving child. Bailey's 'British Directory', 1st edition 1784, lists 'Isaac Beckett and Son' while 'The Staffordshire General and Commercial Directory' (Parson and Bradshaw) 1818 has:—

39

Edward Becket—enameller in Bridge Street.
Isaac Beckett—enamel box and brass-bag lock manufacturer in Duck Lane.
Jane Beckett and Son—tin plate workers, ironbox[5] manufacturers and japanners in Cold Lane.
John Beckett—victualler—The Acorn, Bridge Street.
Benjamin Beckett—baker—Bridge Street.

The later two might have assisted Edward in a part-time capacity. This directory says of Bilston: ' It is principally inhabited by manufacturers of japanned and other wares and colliers employed in the extensive ironworks established here . . . It has been asserted that more iron is made here in Bilston fields than in the whole kingdom of Sweden '.[6] This is looking ahead, however, to when the enamelling trade was rapidly declining.

Another directory, Pigott's 1822/23, has this to say about Bilston: ' The prinicpal trade carried on here besides the iron and coal is japanned and enamelled goods which are got up in great abundance and cheap. Buckle chapes was formerly the staple trade which is still carried on but very much reduced '. Edward Beckett is one of two enamellers named, as he is in the 1828/29 edition; the latter has ' Isaac Beckett iron and tinplate worker in Duck Lane ', while Smart's Directory 1827 also includes ' J. Beckett and Son—japanners of the Bull Holes '; was this Jane, previously in Cold Lane?

The last directory to which reference will be made is ' Bridgen's Directory of Wolverhampton 1833 ' which includes the following:—

Issac and Joseph Beckett—japanners and tinplate workers in Duck Lane.
Mr. Beckett—in Duck Lane.
William Beckett—tinplate worker in Bridge Street.
Benjamin Beckett—baker in Bridge Street.
Mrs. Beckett—boxmaker in Bridge Street.

This Mrs. Beckett was Susanna, the widow of Edward, the enameller, who died in 1831, aged 47 years and was buried in Bilston, 2nd December 1831.

The changes here are significant; as old Isaac aged and became unable to take an active part in the business he retired and became ' a gentleman ' as indicated above. Also in Pigott's Directory for 1829 under ' Gentry and Clergy ' there are only three names and one is ' Isaac Beckett, gent. of Duck Lane '. His nephew Edward took charge and he is the enameller mentioned in the directories for 1818 and 1828. Edward, as indicated, died a few years before his uncle.

Edward Beckett's will proves that enamelling for him had become a rapidly declining trade in the face of new industries and developments. He named his wife as his executrix and instructed her to sell his house in Bridge Street to pay his debts and funeral expenses and then she was to receive what was left, together with his household goods and his cottage-hold property in Duck Lane. His personal estate was sworn at under £100. As Edward Beckett is always listed in Bridge Street, and as there is no reference to the disposal of his tools and equipment in his will, there does not appear to have been much of a business left to support 'widow' Beckett and her four sons and two daughters. The latter did benefit under Isaac the elder's will and, once again, there is an Isaac and an Edward among them.

Old Isaac Beckett who died in 1836 left his premises in Duck Lane to his nephews Isaac and Joseph, sons of Edward the japanner who died in 1803, and occupied by them, but the enamelling work had probably ceased. Other property in Duck Lane and Bridge Street was to be sold. He was able to leave money to many members of the family and Isaac and Joseph each received £150. A comparison of wills is intriguing as indicative of the improvement in the fortunes of the Becketts over a century of trading.

First we have the inventory of the vice maker John Beckett's goods, chattels and personal estate 'as they were taken and appraised by Joseph Perry and Joseph Mousell, the 6th day of January, 1717/18'.

' His wearing apparel '	10s.0d.
One kettle	10s.0d.
One pewter dish	1s.0d.
One warming pan	2s.0d.
An old table	4s.0d.
One bed and furniture	£1. 0s.0d.
An old Pair of bed stocks	2s.0d.
One cow	£2. 0s.0d.
Shopp tools	£2.10s.0d.
Odd things not named	2s.6d.
	£7. 1s.6d.

Contrast this with Isaac Beckett's will of 1836. He has houses, business and land to bequeath, many monetary gifts to make and the total value amounted to nearly £4,000. It would be a reasonable assumption that the foundations of this prosperity were from enamelling. While on the subject of Isaac's will, an interesting bequest worth noting is that of £100 to be employed in founding a Public Dispensary at Bilston, because a few years earlier, in 1832, Bilston had experienced the first dreadful cholera epidemic and the town had been totally unprepared to deal with it. No less than 742 persons died from this disease in that year.

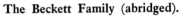

The Beckett Family (abridged).

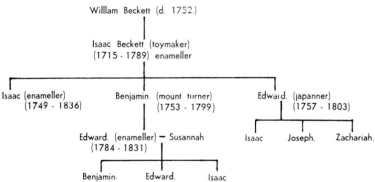

Having examined the family history, we must turn back to the years following 1760 and consider the relationships between the Becketts and another Bilston family, the Prouds. As Isaac was a popular Christian name with the Becketts, so was Samuel with the Prouds and it is not always easy to sort out any particular one.

The family had long been resident in the town, there having been at least three Samuel Prouds in the 17th century, one being the son born to William and Elizabeth Proud in 1689. He also had a son christened Samuel, 1724. Their progress and improvement over the years follows a pattern typical of a number of Bilston families in the 18th century, from Samuel Proud 'cordwainer' (or shoemaker) to Samuel Proud, 'gent'.

The Samuel Proud who died in 1767 had been Constable in

42

Bilston in 1743 and appears as such in the Stowheath Manor Court records. When alterations were being made to the chapel in 1732 we find he was paid 8s.4d. for '500 tiles and carriage '; he was probably acting as the agent. He had adopted his house for the care of 'lunaticks' and this would include the old and feeble. Any such persons among the parish poor might be accommodated by the Overseers in such a ' home ', the owner being paid from the public funds.

The building of a workhouse had been discussed at a vestry meeting in 1737 when Benjamin Bickley was a Chapel Warden and Dovey Hawksford and others agreed to the necessary purchase. It was soon established. At a meeting 22.10.1749., the Overseers agreed that ' Mary, the wife of Caleb Smith shall be taken under the care of Mr. Samuel Proud in order to be cured of her disorder. The Parish agrees to pay 10s.6d. in hand and 5s. per week for the first quarter '.

The burial register has another example as follows—' 7th December 1745. Rev. John, Rector of Elford. He died at Sam Proud's where he had been confined as a lunatick for some time. Died of smallpox '.

This caring for the elderly would appear to have been a common practice, for a certain John Thurstan, surgeon, advertised in Aris' Gazette (3rd August 1752) that he desired ' to acquaint the country that, at Bilston, will be fitted up immediately for the reception of lunaticks a proper house '. This was the man who had been appointed Surgeon and Apothecary to the workhouse by the Overseers in 1743. This advertisement was repeated in the issue of 30th April 1753, but in September 1755, Mr. John Vernon, apprentice to Mr. John Thurstan, surgeon and apothecary at Bilston, took over the house and patients on Thurstan's death.

Another man interested in this early form of nursing-home was Joseph Proud who, in Aris' Gazette of 2nd August 1756, inserted the following: ' Joseph Proud in Bilston—taken a large and convenient house for the reception of lunaticks—the experience he has had by assisting his father, Samuel Proud, who for upwards of 50 years has kept a house for lunaticks— has qualified him to treat that malady '. Joseph was Samuel's younger brother and the Aris' advertisement indicates that it was their father who had begun caring for the feeble in mind or body. Both father

43

and son must have given satisfaction in the service which they provided, for six years later Joseph was advising the public that he 'begs to acquaint the public that he has taken a more commodious house than he had before, for the reception of lunaticks'

Both Samuel and Joseph appear as keepers of 'lunaticks' in the 1781 directory.[7] Yet another Proud engaged in healing would appear from the entry 14.11.1755. 'Mr. John Proud, surgeon, granted £2.2s.0d. for dressing and attendance on an ulcer of the leg of Robert Taylor for 3 months'. In 1761 he was appointed Surgeon and Apothecary for the Workhouse at five guineas a year, but apparently he only officiated for twelve months.

Joseph was not Samuel's eldest son, that was Samuel who died in 1787 and it was the latter's eldest son (another Samuel, who died in 1828) who was decribed as 'proprietor of the Bilston Madhouse'. This seems to indicate that he had taken over from his father, for Joseph Proud had died in 1791 and his premises were advertised to be let in the 'Wolverhampton Chronicle' of 6th June 1792. The same paper (24th August 1791) reported among the deaths 'on Sunday last, at an advanced age, Mr. Joseph Proud, of Bilston, who for many years conducted one of the houses for the reception of lunaticks in that place'. The advertised premises were described as 'A convenient complete House, situated in Bilston, opposite the Church, with parlours, kitchen, chambers, garrets, out offices, walled garden, cold baths and every convenience'.

The Samuel Proud who died in 1828 was Major Proud, who was actively concerned with the local militia during the Napoleonic Wars. His name appears in the Commercial Directory and he was living at Mount Pleasant, close to the church, as late as 1820. The residence must have been of some size for the 1818 levy on it was £14, though this included an additional old house and some plots of land. The present 'Proud's Lane' is also in the immediate vicinity. He was 69 years of age when he died and, no doubt, guided by his father, he had studied medicine and was respected in the town for his work with the mentally sick.

Now we must return to the Becketts, who were related to the Prouds by marriage. Isaac Beckett, the toymaker, had married Hannah Proud in 1737 and their son Isaac Beckett, the enameller, married Ann Proud, the daughter of Joseph, in 1783.[8] Thus,

44

Isaac, the enameller, was both the son-in-law of Joseph and nephew of Samuel the elder. At some time, we know for certain[9] that a number of small oval boxes with a transfer print of the 'madhouse' were made with the words 'Sam Proud' beneath a sketch of the house; above are the words 'A Trifle from Bilston'. These boxes were patch boxes and had a steel mirror inside. One is in the Wolverhampton collection which formerly belonged to Egan Mew.

The transfer is left unpainted but there is a typical Bilston 'pink' enamel round the sides. This box must have been produced in the Beckett workshop and the steel mirror inside the lid is a help in trying to decide which Sam Proud ordered the boxes, which he would give to his friends, those who provided clients or the inmates themselves. As steel mirrors were later replaced by glass we can put the date of this box as between 1770-1780, but when we recall that Sam Proud the elder, died in 1767, then an earlier date—about 1765—seems fairly accurate.

There is an interesting entry in Aris' Gazette for the 8th September 1766, in which is a detailed description of an escaped lunatic from Sam Proud's establishment, but three weeks later another announcement stated that he had been found. The minister of Bilston, Revd. Best, under the date 16th February 1761, records: 'John Guisandarffer, gent. Swiss valet to the Rt. Hon. Earl of Dartmouth'. His senses had become impaired after epileptic fits and he died in the care of Samuel Proud; this indicates not only care for an old servant, but the standing with the public of the Bilston 'madhouse'.

The Becketts probably turned out a great deal of inferior transfer-printed enamels, but, considering their long association with the trade, and the increased knowledge and skill they would acquire over the years, we can say, with some truth, that in the field of individual hand-painted items, some of the finest examples of Bilston enamel work were produced by them, including some of the more unusual-shaped boxes such as bonbonnières. Some of the better transfer-printed pictures may have come from engraved plates by the hand of a local man, John Vardon, who died in 1792. He was also described as a boxpainter and his work is discussed later.

The Beckett workshop must have produced hundreds of

The Beckett and the Proud Families (abridged)

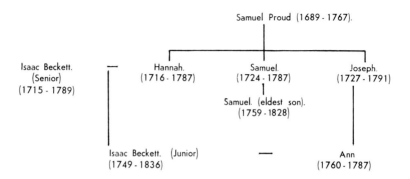

boxes and such items with a transfer print on the lid and single colour enamel on the sides for the home and foreign markets. In their book 'English Painted Enamels',[10] Bernard and Therle Hughes state that Isaac Beckett, the elder, originated the enamelled buckle and specialised in the production of étuis, a necessary item on a lady's dressing table. Hackwood has an interesting observation about old Isaac Beckett, 'The secret of the 'enamel paste' seems to have died with this man, for £1,000 has been offered for it since by a Wolverhampton japanner and met with no response!'[11]

The Becketts perhaps deserve first place among the Bilston enamellers.

REFERENCES

1   S.R.S., 1923. John Beckett exempt from Hearth Tax 1666, p. 62-64.
2   B. Hughes, 'English Snuff Boxes', p. 73.
3   Copy given to me by R. Brettell.
4   11th January 1826.
5   J. Freeman, 'Bilston Almanack Sketches', 1908, p. 21.
6   W. Pitt, 'A Topographical History of Staffordshire', p. 174.
7   J. Freeman, 'Bilston Almanack Sketches', 1908, p. 31. Both in List of Juors, S.R.S., 1947, p. 86.
8   S.R.S., 1931, Wolverhampton Marriage Bonds, p. 13.
9   Gerald Mander, 'The Wolverhampton Antiquary', June 1937.
10 P. 100. Also in 'Collecting Antiques', p. 26.
11 T. W. Hackwood, 'Wednesbury Workshops', p. 19.

6

THE BICKLEY FAMILY

THIS family, like the Becketts, was domiciled in Bilston for over a century and, like the Hawksfords, was very much involved with the affairs of the town and church.

They prospered well over the years but were prepared to join in the business enterprises associated with the exploitation of coal and iron deposits which sprang up with the Industrial Revolution, when enamelling went out of favour.

At the beginning of the eighteenth century, there was, in Bilston, a John Bickley, who was a cordwainer, or cobbler, and who had a small holding, as did many others.[1] He died in September 1706 and the contents of his rooms and barn with his animals was valued at £31.16s.0d.; the value of his wearing apparel and the money in his purse totalled only £1.10s.0d.

John's widow, Susannah, had a hard struggle to bring up her family and when she died, in 1728, all she could leave to her son Benjamin was ' a Bed and chest, 2 pr. of sheets, 2 dishes, 4 plates, the little Brass Pann, a Little Table and the Little Brass Pott '. Benjamin was not her only son for Joseph had been born in 1700. We often read of men who had a poor start in life, but by sheer determination and ability they achieved success and prosperity; Benjamin Bickley belongs to this category.

Benjamin was about three years old when his father died; he was baptised 1st May 1703, and later his mother apprenticed him to a toymaker. [2]On completion of his apprenticeship he set up his own business and must have had ability for there is an entry in the Parish Register recording the death of Sarah Bickley, wife of Benjamin Bickley, toymaker, the 19th September 1729. The following year he was appointed Constable, when only 27 years old. His elder brother Joseph was also established as a toymaker in 1729.

Sarah Gibbons was the first of Benjamin's three wives and could have been related to Edward Gibbons described as a toymaker in 1749 in the Stowheath Manor records. She had been a servant to the Revd. Richard Ames.

Ames has an interesting note in his register regarding this marriage as follows: ' 23rd October 1728. Benjamin Bickley, Toymaker, (at Willenhall) married my head maid Sarah Gibbons much against the consent of her Far. and Mor. However I hope they may do well and I pray God send'em good success '. No doubt he was losing a capable housekeeper. Success came to Bickley, but not to Sarah who died the following year. Her son John was baptised on 20th July 1729, and she was buried on 19th September. Ames described John as ' my Godson ' so there was no ill-feeling over the marriage.

In the Apprentices List we saw Benjamin Bickley described as a toymaker in 1741 and in the short space of ten months he took three apprentices (1743-44) which suggests he was well-established and a well-known manufacturer. These young men were Thomas Harris, William Wilkes and Benjamin Pitt. In addition to being described as a toymaker, Bickley is also called ' chapman ', for instance in an indenture of January 10th 1746. This was something more important than a mere travelling salesman and it is probable that he acted in this capacity for other local business men to some of whom he became related.

Benjamin Bickley's name appears on the first page of the vestry minute book as a Chapel Warden in 1736 when he was 33 and he was re-elected for the two following years. At some stage, with a prosperous toymaking concern, he must have turned to the possibilities of enamelling his goods and he had the means to employ good men. An article in ' The Times ' of 25th May 1963 describes him as Bilston's pioneer enameller. That he was early in the field is seen from a document dealing with a land transaction between himself and John Robins in 1746.[3] In this Bickley has a lease for 21 years of land and buildings with this interesting detail ' with two bays of barning and part of a threshing floor, two cowhouses at the end of the moat, one orchard and two gardens — and also a close — called Millcroft containing about seven acres ', and later on, ' all that toft where an ancient corn mill lately stood, and which is now made and converted into a dwelling house, and all that parcel of land lately covered with water and used as a pool to the aforesaid late mill, but now converted into a meadow'. For this, and other property Bickley was to pay a yearly rental of £16.15s.0d. plus rates. This land was 'bounded by the brook S. and E. and has Doctor Hope's land west and the millcroft north'. It had been in the possession of John Birch and it is interesting to note that Bickley's third wife was a Mary Birch.

Now this property must have been near or adjacant to another one, leased by him in 1748, of about eight acres, and advertised in Aris' Gazette. This was described as having 'a water mill with two overshot wheels, 28ft. high, one part of which hath been used for grinding corn, and the other part is convenient for rolling any kind of metal or boring of gun barrels; there is sufficient room for fixing up spindles for a number of laps, which may be very convenient for several manufactures, exclusive of a complete workshop for twenty pairs of hands'. In addition the notice referred to 'a pair of millstones, two mills for grinding enamels, a dressing mill and several other instruments of a like kind'.

This was obviously not a workshop but a small factory and, among other things, it was producing a good amount of enamel powders. Was this Dovey Hawksford's establishment one is tempted to ask. There are several references in the levies on property owned by the Bickleys for improvements made, for instance:

22.4.1754	Benjamin Bickley 'for the mill $\frac{1}{2}$d.'	
30.4.1756	Benjamin Bickley 'the mill and for the shops $\frac{3}{4}$d.'	
1757	Another $\frac{3}{4}$d. 'for the mill'.	
1758	Another $\frac{1}{4}$d. 'for the mill'.	
1757	John Bickley 'a House' 1s.0d. (a big increase).	
1763	John Bickley 'a shop' $\frac{1}{2}$d.	
1769	John Bickley 'for a house 1d. (inhabited by Joseph Proud) also a reckoning house and a stable'.	

It would appear that Bickley and his son John made their homes in this part of Bilston, still known as Millfields; John's house was called Ettingshall Lodge and had belonged to John Homer of Bromley Hall, Kingswinford, and it is worth noting that Benjamin's son, William, married a Sarah Homer in 1765, though she might have belonged to the Bilston Homer family, also enamellers. The house was on the Sedgley side of the turn-pike road from Bilston, 'near the turn into Gibbet Lane, and much of the surrounding land was owned or leased by Bickley. Iron and steel works were later built on the site.

If Benjamin had a workshop in the heart of Bilston it could have been where he held land off the main street near Homer's Fold. The map shows buildings and gardens fronting the street and a pool is indicated on his land.[5]

Benjamin Bickley must have possessed keen business acumen and at a comparatively early age he was prominent in the town and busily concerned with its affairs. At one time he had a black servant who must have aroused attention in the streets. He was Reuben Massey and in 1753 he ran away; Bickley advertised the fact, gave a description of the man and uttered a warning against re-employing him.[6]

When Richard Ames died in 1758, we find Bickley handling his affairs. He had been a toymaker, japanner and enameller at the premises previously owned by his great uncle, the curate of Bilston. This workshop was at Priestfields and quite close to the Bickley factory. Bickley was also the executor of the will of Dovey Hawksford's mother, in 1756, and he was closely associated with the family; Dovey Hawksford's aunt, Sarah Hawksford, bequeathed to John, son of Benjamin Bickley, £30 when he attained his majority in 1750.

Obviously Benjamin knew all about the work of Dovey Hawksford and, as has been stated, may have taken over his business.

In his later years, Bickley probably took less interest in the enamelling side of his business, but as late as 1775 he is described as a toymaker in a document transferring land to his son John. He bought up property with coal or other mineral possibilities and was interested in the new industrial developments taking place. He married three times, his second wife being Margaret Gibbons, the sister of his first wife Sarah; she died in 1762. Margaret did not marry Benjamin at either Bilston or Wolver-hampton, but probably Willenhall, like her sister. She bore the following children, William 1735, Benjamin 1737, Elizabeth 1739, Benjamin 1741, Thomas 1744 and Francis 1746; of these William was the important survivor. Sarah and Margaret were the

50

daughters of William Gibbons of Ettingshall who lived near part of the Bickley property; Bickley stated this in his will when, referring to his son William, he wrote 'son of the late deceased Margaret, the youngest daughter of William Gibbons, heretofore of Ettensall'. Also in that locality was Edward Gibbons, described as 'gent' in his will proved 26th April 1743. If these two were related, then Bickley would appear to have married into a family with money, for Edward Gibbons left £600 to his son Thomas, £330 to each of his four daughters, and other beneficiaries were his wife Mary and son William. The inventory of his personal estate amounted to £397.10s.0d.

Bickley's third wife was Mary Birch whom he married in 1766.[7] She was a widow and survived him, dying in 1780; she may have been related to Matthew Birch, recorded as a toymaker in 1750.

Bickley died in January 1776, a prosperous man and described as 'gentleman' in a power of attorney of that year. In his will there is only one actual amount mentioned, that is £500 bequeathed to Elizabeth, widow of John Hood of Bristol; Elizabeth was the daughter of his second wife, Margaret Gibbons. He desired his estate to be shared equally between his sons John and William, after making provision for his wife. He names William as his executor and writes, 'I hereby acknowledge to be my son, and who was registered by the name of William, son of Benjamin and Margaret Bickley'. This was, apparently to legitimatize and legalize his birth. Benjamin in his will left 'the rest and remainder of leasehold lands and buildings, money and securities for money, stock-in-trade, book debts, household goods and chattels and personal estate to son John Bickley and afs'd. William'. Three other sons had died in infancy.

John Bickley must have worked, as a young man, in his father's business for a directory of 1770 describes him as an enamelled boxmaker and he and his step-brother William benefited from their father's enterprises. John is also described as a chapman — like his father — and the court Rolls of Stowheath Manor contain many references to land dealings in which he was involved during the period 1755-1768. From December 1766 to March 1772 there are 28 entries relating to John Bickley alone— extensive dealings in land and minerals. In 1759 he was appointed

51

to collect the Land Tax. He had an eye to exploiting the coal seams in the area, and in his will he is described as a coalmaster. He also set up one of the earliest blast furnaces in Bilston, following the lead of John Wilkinson.

In April 1769 he advertised as follows:—

'To be sold to the best bidder on the 4th May next, at the house of William Lewis, the new Bull's Head in Bilston, a copyhold estate held of the Manor of Stowheath and situate in Bilston, consisting of three well built houses fronting the principal street and opposite to the Red Lion Inn, with barns, gardens etc. and two pews in Bilston Chapel—now held by the said John Bickley only, also six tenements standing behind the said front houses and let to the said John Bickley who holds the same with the premises first described at the yearly rent of 50 guineas. The premises are very compact, being nearly surrounded by a moat'.

The rent represents a considerable sum and the description is helpful in trying to picture the main street in Bilston, with its assortment of houses, shops, workshops and gardens with fields immediately beyond.

Two years later, John offers for sale 'a piece of land with a good coal mine under it, near 3 acres, adjoining to the town street in Bilston'. It is worth noting that the Town Hall, built later at the junction of Church Street and Lichfield Street was erected over a very thick coal seam.

In the Levy Book of 1770 which gives the principal land-owners in the town John Bickley had a total of 111 acres.[8] He still had an interest in farming it appears, for in April 1766 he advertises that he has on offer 'very good flax seed for sowing and a quantity of Chutered Flax'. Flax had probably been grown on land near Ettingshall Lodge, for there were flax ovens there.

In 1773 he informed the public that he has 20 acres of land 'in which is a ten yard coal, considerably nearer Birmingham than any other colliery on the Birmingham canal' and he wants financial backing for 'erecting a fire engine etc, for getting the said mines'. The following year he advertises 'a large wharf, with warehouse, near the canal in Wolverhampton now open for business and the sale of coal and coke'. An act for making a canal between Bilston and Birmingham had been passed in 1768 and part of the line ran quite close to the Bickley home at Ettingshall Lodge. In 1793 Bickley's executors put up for auction '30 or 40 acres of very rich ironstone mine' through which ran the Birmingham Canal. The opening of this canal reduced the cost of transporting coal to Birmingham from Bilston from 13 shillings to 8s.4d. a ton.[9] By the year 1792 Wolverhampton already had a Canal Street and boat builders and boatmen are named in the directory.

Like his father, he had some servant trouble, for in September 1776 he warns[10] against any persons employing his articled servant Charles Griffiths, who had absconded. Also troubled was his widow; it was reported in June 1792 that 'John Morred, who had decamped with upwards of £100 of Mrs. Bickley's of Ettingshall, was apprehended at Bromsgrove, with the greater part of the money in his possession and conveyed to gaol'.

It would appear then that enamelling was only one of John Bickley's interests if, perhaps, the main one of his father, but he only outlived Benjamin by a matter of months, dying in the same year, October 1776. He died a rich man, for apart from making good provision for his widow Catharine he left £1,000 to each of his children, unnamed, when they came of age and £40 to each of two servants. He also directed that 'as many of my boats shall be sold as shall be sufficient to pay my debt to Mr. William Kaye', further evidence of his involvement in the coal and coal-transport business.[11] One of his executors named, in addition to his widow, was John Bracebridge Hawksford, the same relative who, in his own will (1793) left £100 to Catharine, his cousin, and to each of her sons Benjamin and William and to her two daughters, Sarah and Mary Ann.

John Bickley married his wife, Catharine Smith, in 1758[12] when she was only 19 years old. Their offspring were Sarah (1759), Benjamin (1763), Catharine (1767), and William (1768) and finally Mary Ann.

On the 30th December 1776 notice was given of the 'lease of a Mill at Bilston to be sold, mills for grinding enamel, also house, late in the occupation of Benjamin Bickley, dec'd. Apply William Bickley in Bilston'.

Also at the end of December 1776 the sale of John Bickley's stock-in-trade was advertised in the Aris' Gazette and noted as 'consisting of Tools and Utensils for carrying on the enamel business—and also many valuable sets of patterns now in the hands of some of the first merchants in the Kingdom from which considerable orders may be expected '. This latter indicates his activities as a chapman. He was only 47 years old when he died.

The year 1777 saw the approaching end of the Bickley family's prime interest in enamelling, though the 1781 Directory lists widow Bickley as an enamelled boxmaker. This was Catharine, John's widow. The same directory mentions ' Bickley and Molineux—wharfingers of Stafford Street, Wolverhampton '. This could have been Benjamin's other son William who had been involved in the family business activities. William, in 1765, at the age of 30, had married a Bilston girl—Sarah Homer. He may have been more interested in japanning, however, for he is called a japanner in 1776[13] and also in his stepmother's will we have ' To William Bickley—japanner £10 '. She referred to four houses with shops, gardens and so forth, let to tenants for him to deal with, part of Benjamin's accumulated property. He was also prominent in Bilston Chapel affairs for in 1780 he was dealing with plans and tenders for re-roofing the church. A few years later we find him (1788) concerned with the Bilston Association for the prosecution of felons.

He left a substantial fortune when he died in 1798. His daughter Margaret, deceased, had received £1,000 on her marriage and £1,000 was secured for her issue. William's son—William Homer Bickley—died a bachelor in 1802, and intestate, and the two sisters-in-law, Sarah and Catharine, are named in a bond on the same document, in which Sarah claims his estate which was sworn at under £1,000.

Catharine Bickley survived till 1814; she benefited in the will of her cousin Mary Ames who died at her home in 1782. She received £20 and each of her five children (Sarah, Benjamin, Catharine, William S. and Mary Ann) £10. Some clothing and jewellery was also bequeathed to them. She had allowed some of her husband's property to be sold to raise money.

In March 1778, timber near Bilston (including 66 oak, 31 ash and other trees) growing ' on land in the holding of Mrs. Bickley ' was advertised and later in the same year shares in property at Bilston were offered. The next year a meadow with coal under it was for sale and a field with coal, ironstone and clay under it was put up for sale in 1788. With her other executors of John's will she offered, in 1793, 30 to 40 acres at Catchem's

Corner, Ettingshall, a very rich ironstone mine.

Benjamin, Catharine's son, became a Bristol merchant, while William went to America and we find no further references to enamelling after her. The Staffordshire General and Commercial Directory for 1818 mentions only one Bickley, W. S. Bickley, described as gentleman, of Meynel House, near Bilston. In the 1771 Survey, this area was owned by John Bickley and the house was built in his, or his son's time. John Freeman states that the Bickley residence stood on the west side of Willenhall Road.[14] Another home was what he calls the Old Hall. He adds that a descendant, Latty Bickley, lived here as a local squire and he acquired a reputation as a sportsman and something of an eccentric. It was in the vicinity of Market Street, where there used to be a row of houses with the front done in Bilston stone and called the Stone Building, originally part of the Old Hall. Freeman may be wrong about Latty Bickley's home, for the 1832 list of Contributors to the Cholera appeal has:— 'Bickley, J. L. Esq., of Ettingshall Lodge'. This suggests he was living in his grandfather's John Bickley's house.

The Wolverhampton Directory of 1827 has 'Bickley, Danks and Co. boats and wharves at Horseley Fields, Wolverhampton'. This firm was engaged in the River Severn trade. It also names a William Bickley of Millfields, Bilston, but no trade is given. Could this be the William who went to America, described in John Bracebridge Hawksford's will of 1793 as 'lately gone to America'?

Meynel House continued to be a Bickley residence for William's daughter Katharine lived and died there (1832) and he himself died there in 1842 aged 74 years, his estate being sworn at under £1,000.

In the 1833 directory he is called 'Captain Bickley, of Meynel House, Cold Lanes', while the obituary notice of his death describes him as 'formerly Captain of the Bilston troop of Yeomanry Cavalry'. One is left with the thought that he may have been with Wellington's troops at the battle of Waterloo! In his later years he became a farmer for he owned some acres near his home. The same directory mentions a John Bickley who was a surveyor in Bride's Row, on the road to Willenhall.

Reference to the enamel work of the Bickleys is made later

on but, in conclusion, it may be stated that it was Benjamin Bickley who established the business, that his sons helped to develop it and that before the end of the century both the trade and Bilston had been deserted by some of the family for more salubrious places.

The Bickley Family (abridged)

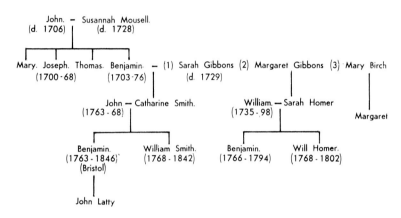

REFERENCES
1 He was Church Warden 1706.
2 Kate Foster in her 'Scent Bottles', p. 54, says that it was Joshua Devey, Wolverhampton toymaker, 1741. This cannot be correct.
3 Hand Morgan Collection, W.S.L. B. and T. Hughes, 'English Painted Enamels', pp. 88 and 98.
4 A. Barnet, 'History of Lower Gornal', Sed. R.L., p. 23.
5 J. Freeman, 'Bilston Almanack Sketches', 1916, p. 35. Reference to a large pond in Greencroft.
6 Aris' Gazette.
7 S.R.S., 1931. Wolverhampton Marriage Bonds.
8 Price, p. 89, gives a list of land owned by John Bickley at the 1771 Survey and pieces rented on other pages.
9 J. A. Langford, 'A Century of Birmingham Life', p. 178.
10 Aris' Gazette.
11 C. Hadfield, 'The Canals of the West Midlands', Chapter 4.
12 S.R.S., 1931. Wolverhampton Marriage Bonds.
13 Also in List of Jurors, S.R.S., 1947, p. 86.
14 J. Freeman, 'Bilston Almanack Sketches', 1916, pp. 11-13.

7

OTHER BILSTON ENAMELLERS

IT has been suggested that some of the men who had been engaged in such trades as toymaking, boxmaking, or buckle-making may have turned to enamelling as an attractive means of enhancing their business, that is beautifying their copper objects in their own workshops. This could have occurred at any time from about 1750 onwards. Another possibility is that a son or other relative, or even a valued assistant, might be left a shop and tools in a will and subsequently attempt to do enamel work.

There was a big demand for enamelled pieces both at home and abroad, the most productive period in Bilston being about 1760-1785 when the techniques of transfer-printing and the application of an increasing range of colours were fully mastered. Apart from the demands of the home market, there was a good trade connection with European countries and the developing American States. French and other continental innovations regarding objects and designs were readily copied in a cheaper form.[1]

With regard to Bilston, it must be noted that the better-off masters and their families were often connected by marriages, sons marrying daughters and vice-versa. They knew what friends and rivals were doing, discussed problems and arranged for a chapman to advertise their wares and extend their trade. The master enameller could obtain, if necessary, his trinkets and boxes from a neighbour who shaped the copper objects on his premises. Hinges for boxes, mounts and copper plaques were available locally; colours could now be purchased in powder form ready for use, for instance from Birmingham, where it will be recalled as early as 1751, Abraham Seaman advertised[2] that he was making and selling ' all sorts of enamelling colours ' and, on his death, his widow continued the business.

PERRY

IT is difficult to sort out the numerous Perrys in Bilston in the 18th century, but one branch had been long established in the town and is of some importance.

When the chantry chapel of St. Leonard was founded in 1458, a William Perry was one of 15 householders who surrendered land to endow it, and the Revd. Ames notes that Clement Perry, son of William Perry, of the Corner House, was priest in Bilston from 1531 to 1556 at least. Lawley says that the same Clement was a native of Bilston[3] and became priest when the chapel was re-opened in the 4th year of Queen Mary (1557). A rent roll of Elizabeth's reign contains five men named Perry and the Hearth Tax Returns for 1673 has the following:—

William Perry de Gate	4	(died 1711).
John Perry	5	
Perry de Croft ...	6	(died 1703).
Perry de Corner ...	4	

This suggests substantial homes. The 1665-6 Returns show an exemption for

Thomas Perry ...	6	
Thomas Perry ...	1	(for his smithy).

These Perry homes were solidly-built Tudor houses and still in family use into the eighteenth century. The ' de Corner ' one was at the corner of today's Wood Street; the ' de Croft ' was near the present ' Greencroft ' and probably disappeared when the G.W.R. railway cutting was made; the ' de Gate ' may have been near the present Market Street, or close to Greencroft.[4]

One section of the Perrys were Catholics; Clement Perry, son of William of the Corner House, was trained at Halesowen Monastery in Worcestershire, and as he was priest in Bilston in the reign of Mary,[5] this suggests that it was the descendants of this family who were Catholics. When Bishop Lloyd made his survey and inspection of the parishes in the Lichfield diocese, in the last decade of the 17th century, he mentions that there were about ten families of dissenters in Bilston and these included some Perrys. A list of Papists in the town in 1705 contains John Perry, his wife Mary and four children, Thomas Perry, Mary his wife and two children, Joseph Perry junior's wife Elizabeth and two daughters. The Revd. Best records Elizabeth Perry's burial, 30th September 1737, as the wife of a Catholic.

Another Perry similarly noted by Best was Joseph senior who was, however, a flax dresser. He could have been the man, together with Edward Perry, who witnessed the will of old John Bickley when he died in 1707, suggesting they were neighbours or business associates. Some Catholics refused to take the oath of allegiance to George I on his accession in 1714, and one such was 'Thomas Perrye, Locksmith' who was fined £13.13s.0d. In October 1727 Ames buried another Catholic—'Mrs. Mary Perry, widow de Gate, Roman Catholic'.

In attempting to discover which particular Perrys were the ancestors of the enameller we are helped by the fact that some members moved out of the town, while in other families the male line became extinct. Humphrey Perry died at Stafford in 1716, a 'man of much wealth' says Lawley.[6] He died without leaving any issue. He left £100 from his copyhold estate in Bilston for the provision of a new house for the curate and also financial assistance for placing poor children as apprentices to 'Some Honest Trade or Calling for the Term of Seven Yeares at least', such children to be at least fourteen years old. Ames also records that in 1726 Edward Perry of 'ye Corner House' moved to Wolverhampton. Three Perrys are recorded on tablets in St. Leonard's Church for their generosity in various ways, and some had close connections with the church. We find a Thomas Perry serving with Dovey Hawksford as Chapel Warden for the Liberty of Bilston in 1731 and 1732, and an Alexander Perry, gentleman, in 1733.

Thomas was a bucklemaker who died in 1763. He was not the Thomas born to George and Catharine Perry in 1702, but William's son, for he is so designated when Mary, his daughter was born in 1720. George's son had been a pupil of Ames and after graduating at Baliol College, Oxford, he was ordained Deacon by the Bishop of Worcester in 1725 at his palace at Hartlebury. He apparently had no male children living, for he left his household goods, shop tools and so forth to his son-in-law, Joseph Mills, but the total value of the estate was only £18.15s.0d.

In 1725 Thomas Perry, described as a toymaker, took James

and William Pool as apprentices until they reached the age of 24 years,[7] and this may be the Thomas Perry who was Parish Clerk, says the Revd. Best, for 37 years, while a Humphrey Perry was occupying the same office in 1774 and up to his death in 1781.

From the numerous Perry entries in the Parish Register among the fathers, in addition to Thomas we have Joseph Perry, a toymaker, William, a chape-forge maker and bucklemaker, George, a toymaker, Peter, a bucklemaker. The Revd. Ames made an entry under 6th August 1728 to the effect that he was a bearer at the funeral of his old friend Edward Perry. This would seem to be the same man of whom he made another entry under 15th March 1726 to report 'Edward Perry of ye Corner gent. removed to Wolverhampton'. He had been a great friend of the curate who frequently added a little additional information about the better-off inhabitants of his parish. He had conducted Edward's marriage to Mrs. Mary Pipe, a member of a prominent Bilston family, in 1702, but states that they went to live in Birmingham. However their son Thomas was baptised in Bilston in 1705, and Mary's death is recorded in 1707; she was buried in 'my Lord Bradford's Chancell in Wolverhampton Church', Thomas, Edward's son, was also at Baliol College, graduating in 1726 and admitted to Deacon's Orders; he had likewise been a pupil of the curate. Edward died in 1728 at Wolverhampton aged nearly 60 years and his son only outlived him by a few days.

A list of pew owners in 1733 contains the names of Joseph Perry, Alexander Perry (of the Gate House) and Thomas Perry (here described as a bucklemaker)[8] and, from the additional facts that George Perry is called a toymaker in 1748 (he died in 1772) and that Joseph was a toymaker, who in 1750 was dead, for his widow Elizabeth sold land to Samuel Proud, we can come nearer to establishing who were the 'Perry and Sons' listed as enamellers in the 1770 directory, and the Thomas Perry described as an enamelled boxmaker in that of 1781. Moreover, Bailey's British Directory of 1784 has Mary Perry—enameller in general.

Thomas, the son of George, the toymaker, is the probability; he was born in 1737 and in 1767 he took an apprentice to learn enamel painting. He died in 1808 and in his will dated 1782 he

60

is called an enameller. Mander says that Thomas Perry died in 1808 'having made a bare livelihood, out of his business which seems, nevertheless to have continued.[9] His eldest son was also named Thomas and the will was witnessed by John Perry and George Perry, but it was sworn at under £100.

Another man to be considered is Edward Perry, the son of Joseph, the toymaker, who in 1760 was living at the 'Gate of Green Croft'. The custom of giving a newborn son the same Christian name as that of a son who died in infancy is fairly common. Joseph named a son Edward in 1746 and another in 1748. This latter is probably the young man who served an apprenticeship with Penelope Carless who was a boxpainter (June 1762), and then set up his own business in the town.

In their book 'English Painted Enamels', Bernard and Therle Hughes state that George Stubbs, R.A. worked, at one time, in the Perry factory, but this could not be the celebrated artist who became internationally famed amongst other work for his painting of horses. The following entry appears in the Wednesbury Parish Register:—' 1752, March 22. George Stubbs of Huntington, near Cannock, son of Mr. Francis Stubbs and Beatrice, d. of the late Mr. John Cox of Wednesbury, married to Anne Butler, d. of Mr. John Butler of Wednesbury. Mr. George Stubbs was under my care for several years at Bilston '. This was written by the Revd. Edward Best who might well have arranged for one of the Perrys, with whom he was closely associated, to take the boy, but the date would suggest little knowledge of enamelling by Stubbs.

The trade would continue in the family for many years, for in the Staffordshire General and Commercial Directory for 1818 there appears the name of George Perry, enameller, who had his premises in Temple Street. This indicates that, despite a marked decline in the trade, the Perry business continued, apparently in new premises in a developing part of the town, Newtown, as it was called. Here, too, James Perry was engaged in the allied trade of japanning while Mary Perry, gentlewoman, was residing in the old part of the town in Church Street. She was probably the enameller of 1784 now living in comfortable retirement.

In 1825, a Thomas Perry lent £290 towards the re-building of St. Leonard's Church.[10] Thomas Perry had established an

61

ironworks in the Bradley area of Bilston at Highfields. In the same year, the Wesleyan Church trustees purchased the hall and lands of the late Mr. Joseph Perry, situated at the top of Oxford Street, for their new chapel. This probably was not the residence of the old Perrys de Corner for, on the other hand, in 1781 Joseph Perry had been a 'keeper of the lunaticks' so his house is a possible origin. It became for a short time, after his death in 1820, a public house.

SMITH

THE 1770 and 1781 Directories both give the name of Isaac Smith as an enamelled box-maker, but such a common surname creates difficulties in trying to trace a particular descent.

The Revd. Ames' register gives us a Joseph Smith (buckle-maker), Thomas Smith (locksmith) and John Smith (bucklemaker and chaper) but no box-maker or toy-maker. Thomas Smith was born in 1688, the son of William Smith and his wife Elizabeth. Ames goes to the trouble to write that she was the daughter of Edward Homer of Ettingshall, indicating some certain standing, in his eyes at least. The Homers are discussed later. One of the most prominent of the Smiths, however, would appear to have been William Smith, who was a prosperous baker; for two periods, 1731-33 and 1745-49, he was a Chapel Warden. He had married Catharine Hawksford, at Bilston, in 1724 and so was related to Dovey Hawksford. His daughter Catharine married John Bickley and she had learned, at some time in her life, enough about enamelling to carry on the business after her husband's death in 1776, possibly with the advice and help of relatives.

William Smith died in 1755 and his estate totalled £391, and it was his widow who is referred to in an advertisement of 2nd April 1762 requesting all debts owing to be paid to Mr. John Bickley, her son-in-law, or Mr. Edward Kempson, she having recently died.

Thomas Smith the locksmith, was William's brother; he died in 1729 leaving a son William, but in 1752 we find the Revd Best recording the birth of a son, Thomas Smith, 'to Thomas, gent. brother to my wife, and Mary, his wife'. The parson was a godfather, but the child did not survive. Thomas Smith died in

1781 and would appear to have left no male issue and probably he had no connection with the enamelling trade.

We now come to a John Smith, who was apprenticed to William Cox of Wolverhampton, as a ' painter ' in 1753. Cox is described as a boxpainter in 1756 and painter in 1762 and 1763 and he could have done work in enamelling and japanning. This Smith may have been the son of John Smith, the bucklemaker, and he probably carried on similar work after completing his apprenticeship. The Isaac Smith of the directories could not have been his son because of the dates involved. He was possibly the son of John Smith, chape forger, baptized 24th November 1726.

Isaac and Sarah Smith had a son born in 1764 whom they had christened Isaac and the register has an Isaac Smith, married to Elizabeth (1748) and Margaret (1750 and 1757 entries). It could be the same man; Benjamin Bickley, for instance, had three wives. This and other Smiths tend to cloud the issue, but whatever the family members involved it seems probable that the development was from buckle and chape making to box making and enamelling, with help and support from other family connections in the trade. A Samuel Smith in 1781 is described as a watch-chain maker and one is inclined to surmise that he made little chains for the enamelled wine labels on occasions. That this family business continued for a long period may be concluded from the fact that a John Smith had a japanning and tinplate work in Church Street in 1833.

HOMER

THERE was more than one family with the name Homer, but none long-established in the town. The Chief Rent Book of 1699 shows a Thomas Homer ' for land bought of Perry ',[11] Elizabeth Homer, widow, and Henry Homer. They are called, with others, ' newcomers ' and they probably came from Walsall. On the other hand, there were Homers just outside the Bilston Parish boundary at Ettingshall (in Sedgley Parish) and the latter registers mention the following:—

| ' Francis Homer of Ettingshall | locksmith | 13. 8.1688. |
| Edward Homer of Ettingshall | yeoman | 10.12.1677.' |

The latter's will of that date refers to ' land in Ettingshall and

Bilston ' and land in ' Bilston Field '; his personal estate realised £235.15s.0d. and mentions Edward, the eldest son, and Thomas. Edward continued in business in Ettingshall; he was there in 1712. His daughter Elizabeth married into the Smith family of Bilston in 1687.

The Homers are another instance of the progress from one form of metal work to another and to at least one member becoming an enameller.

In the early decades of the 18th century, a Thomas Homer is described as a locksmith and Edward Homer as a gunlock maker. In 1727, Ames baptized Edward Homer, son of Edward the second, a locksmith. Both would appear to have been successful and in the Church Accounts, Thomas is twice described as ' gent. '. His name also occurs in documents relating to exchanges of land in Bilston open fields between William Robins and others; these include pieces in Colepitt Field and Windmill Field.

Thomas Homer married a grand-daughter of Esther Dovey and here again is another link-up with the boxmakers, toymakers and enamellers; he died in 1761, but he may not have been directly involved in the enamel trade. However, in 1723, William Homer who came from Walsall was apprenticed to Dovey Hawksford[12] to learn the craft of toymaker and through family connections he knew the local men engaged in engraving, boxpainting and enamelling; his son married into the Bickley family, to Elizabeth, daughter of William Bickley, and his daughter Sarah married William, the younger son of Benjamin Bickley.

It is this William, Hawksford's apprentice, who became an enameller—and one of the earliest in Bilston. John Freeman, in his book ' Wesleyan Methodism in Bilston ',[13] mentions that Wesley visited the town in 1745 and soon afterwards several people offered their homes for meetings; one of these was ' Mr. Homer, the enameller of Homer's Fold '.[14] Even if we interpret the phrase ' soon after ' as a few years later this would still place him among the earliest enamellers. It is interesting to note that in the Bilston collection of enamels there is a medallion portrait of John Wesley, in a frame about $3\frac{1}{2}''$ across. One is tempted to think this came from Homer's workshop.

In the year before Wesley's visit, William's membership of the Established Church is seen in the fact that he paid 11 guineas for pew number 31 when pews in the new gallery were offered for sale.[15]

His house and others behind it formed the ' fold '—a collection of three-storey houses forming a kind of square fronting Church Street and west of the present Greencroft. The site has been cleared, but the 1842 schedule of lands in Bilston details the area to which a later Homer (Benjamin) had admittance and it had almost certainly undergone little change since William's time. It consisted of ' a house, brewhouse, warehouse and yard fronting the street; house, warehouse and shop with yard also fronting the street, at the Corner of Homer's Fold, four small houses with a yard in common, fourteen houses with stable and workshop '.

William Homer was probably the man of that name sworn in as Constable in October 1754—an important office—and the Land Survey of 1771 shows him renting a beanfield of some acres. He died in 1777,[16] shortly after the two Bickleys, father and son, and in his will he is described as a ' chapman ', a term we have seen applied to John Bickley and Dovey Hawksford. There is a reference to property in Walsall which helps to identify him with the William Homer apprenticed to Hawksford in 1723. He left £150 to each of his daughters, Mary Sylvester and Sarah Bickley, and £300 to his unmarried daughter Elizabeth. A son William, who was born in 1737, is also named. We may conclude that he was a successful enameller, although his name does not appear in the 1770 directory. As a member of the closely-connected family groups of toymakers, enamellers and others, he, no doubt, had the benefit of their technical ' know-how ', sources of materials, outlets and so forth.

A small incident of mutual assistance is seen in 1765 when, as a result of a Chancery suit, £126 was owed to the widow of William Green and parishioners advanced loans to meet it. These included William Homer, Benjamin Bickley and Thomas Smith for £5 each, and Samuel Stone for £10.

Others of the Homers who had been called ' newcomers ' settled on the outskirts of the town in the Ettingshall area. Richard Homer, of Ettingshall Lane, was a gunlocksmith and when he died, in 1767, leaving a son Richard only 11 years old, he left his shop tools and utensils to his wife Mary, until his eldest son Benjamin was 21. Another Homer settled in the same area was

Edward, who was a prosperous gunlockmaker and had a son Edward born in 1753. This son is, in all probability, the 22 year old sailor buried in December 1775.

The gunlocksmith married Mary Kemsey in 1743, and when he died in 1778 he left £60 to his eldest son Kemsey and £40 to his son Harry, his wife being chief beneficiary. It is difficult to sort out the various Homers in the Parish Register as the same names recur: two Edwards died in 1778 and two Benjamins in 1783 and 1784. The latter were father and son, the younger being a bachelor.

The Mary Homer above, Richard's widow, could not have been Mary who died in 1752, the latter was certainly not the mother of Edward above (born in 1753), but her daughter. Elizabeth Homer married into another family prominent in Bilston, with connections with the enamellers, that of Samuel Stone. This Mary Homer, described as a widow in her will, signed with her mark, had inherited a small, but thriving, business from her husband for she was able to leave £10 to her sons Edward and William, £30 to Thomas and £20 to Benjamin and a legacy to her daughter Elizabeth Stone. Another son, John, is named as an executor, but there is no other reference to him in the will, except that he was to receive a guinea.

The Land Survey of 1771 also mentions a Benjamin Homer who rented several pieces of land. He was apparently a butcher by trade and he died in 1784. There is also a Mrs. Homer who had some 28 acres of land in all, two pieces of which Benjamin rented.

It is possible that enamelling was superseded by japanning in the Homer workshop, for Bailey's ' British Directory of 1784 ' contains reference to ' Homer and Bickley—japanners ', and, by this date, William Homer and both Benjamin and John Bickley were both dead. Another indication of the change is that in her will (1780) Mary Bickley, Benjamin's widow, left two guineas to William Homer, japanner, ' for mourning '.

AMES

REFERENCE has been made to our indebtedness to the Revd. Richard Ames for his Parish Register with his comments and observations. Coming to Bilston in 1684, he seems to have settled happily in the town with his mother, secured the support of the gentry and business men, such as the Hawksfords, and interested himself in the business enterprises of the town. This is evident from the fact that at one time he had three nephews from the north of the county working in Bilston.

In a document of 1717[17] dealing with transfers of land held by the old and well-to-do family of Robins we find the following: 'Richd. Ames holds part of a messuage, house with a Garden Paddock meadow, 2 orchards, stable and cow-house and the great Bay of the Barn with privilege of the Threshing Bay'. This would be near the church, but part of the church land was, from old time, situated at Priestfields, and the curate had a workshop there where japanning, and later enamelling, was carried on, for he mentions that his nephews John and Joseph Ames began to work in the shop in 1729.[18]

The curate was obviously pleased to have his nephews in Bilston for he puts a memorandum in the Baptisms Register as follows: '18th April 1729, Memd. that 26th March last my nephews John and Joseph Ames began to work in the Shoppe of my house at Priestfields'. Ames adds that Joseph and Benjamin Stephens went to live there, perhaps as workmen, and his servant Mary Beavon, who was to act as housekeeper, one assumes. The house and workshop would be on the church property and previously let to some tenants; William Ames had improved the premises. This elder brother William, however, had been in Bilston earlier than this and graduated to toymaker.

From April 1716 onwards, the curate indicated the occupation of the father in the Register of Baptisms and not the mother's name; when he recorded the birth of 'Elizabeth, daughter of William Ames (my nephew)' he called him a bucklemaker in 1718, but a whitesmith in 1716.

William died in 1784. He apparently married twice, his first wife being Elizabeth Hawksford, Dovey's sister, who died in 1757, the same year as his son's wife, Margaret. The first three months of the year were grievious in Bilston, for Ames records many deaths which he could only describe as being from 'putrid fever' or 'flux and fever'. As noted, William married into the Hawksford family and, no doubt, he came under the influence of Dovey and others who could assist him financially or technically. Ames has the following entry: 'on 28th October 1715 my nephew William Ames, was married to Elizabeth, ye eldest d. of Richard Hawksford of Bilston, yeoman, by Catharine his wife'. He was Constable in 1723.

He had a son Richard, born in 1716 who may be referred to as Richard Ames the Younger. This boy would not have to seek a master and pay a substantial sum to be taken on as an apprentice since he could learn all about the business from his father and relatives.

He took over the Priestfields workshop eventually and is described as a toymaker. With japanned work going on at the same time it is logical to assume that the copper 'toys' and so forth being produced were, before long, treated with enamelling in the workshop, even if Ames did not do the work himself. However he did take apprentices such as William Cox in 1743 and Thomas Bayliss. These were boxpainters and since Bayliss witnessed his will, he could well have been employed by him.

Richard Ames died in 1758; his wife had died earlier, in the previous year, and now two young daughters, Margaret and Mary were left orphans. His sons Richard, Joseph and Dovey all had pre-deceased him, the latter two dying within weeks of each other in 1749; also a daughter Elizabeth passed away in 1755. In his will, Ames requested 'his shops, gardens, pieces of land, meadow or pasture etc. at Priestfields to be sold by his cousin, John Bracebridge Hawksford on behalf of his two daughters, Margaret and Mary'.

This property would be less than a mile from Bilston's main street and the use of the plural suggests more than one type of work. It can be assumed that Ames added to his great uncle's original workshop, which was somewhat isolated, for, from the 1771 Survey, we find that four fields called Priestfields belonged to the living of Penkridge and four to the living of Stretton; in addition the Revd. Best, who succeeded the Revd. Ames, (the first's nephew who became curate in 1730) was renting five pieces to Hawksford. Coal was easily available on these sites.

The family rallied round on Richard Ames' death and Benjamin Bickley attended to debts owing to him. It is not known who took over the workshops—perhaps Bayliss—for there was no son to follow as two had died in infancy. However, it will be recalled that two of his father's brothers—John and Joseph—had also come to Bilston in 1729 and begun work at Priestfields and his father too appears to have outlived him. Therefore there could have been a continuation of the work at Priestfields or in Bilston.

A John Ames was certainly married and settled in Bilston as early as 1732 and several children were born to his wife Sarah in the years to 1743. The Revd. Ames, the Younger, made no special reference in the register. Also a Joseph Ames married Catharine Salt in 1747. The parish was not given at the time, unless one of the pair lived outside Wolverhampton, yet a few months later Ann Salt ' of Bilston ' married a Birmingham man. These girls were obviously related to John Salt who was a box-maker (1721) and toymaker (1726). All this, it must be remembered, pre-dates Richard's death and the two brothers could have returned to North Staffordshire or moved to a place such as Birmingham. There is no mention of the name Ames in the Land Survey already referred to, and the business changed hands and possibly ceased, for this part of Bilston rapidly developed as a coal-mining area with ironworks.

Whatever enamel work was done by Ames it would consist largely of individual hand-painted pieces since he died before the technique of transfer printing could have been successfully mastered and practised in Bilston.

It was stated above that John Bracebridge Hawksford was the executor of Ames' will and he acted in the same capacity for Mary Ames, who, having left Bilston for St. Mary-le-Bone, Middlesex, in her will dated 1778, (she died in 1782) desired to be buried ' in the chancel of the church of Bilston, as near to the remains of my dear mother as may be '. Her will contains a number of references to Hawksfords and Bickleys and bequests are made to the three daughters and son (John) of her uncle William Ames and to the two daughters of ' Cousin Richard Ames '.

Mary Ames was a spinster and apparently the daughter of

69

Richard Ames who entered the Church and married Sarah Hawksford, daughter of Richard Hawksford; he followed his uncle as a curate at Bilston in 1730, coming from Stretton-upon-Dunsmore, Warwickshire. His wife died in 1732, leaving him with a young daughter—the above Mary—and this explains the expressed wish to be buried in the chancel of the Church. Under 16th July 1731, Ames wrote in the Register of Baptisms: ' Mary d. of Richard Ames, curate at Bilston '. This was Richard Ames, the Younger, for his uncle had died in 1730 as already mentioned. The register shows that another Mary Ames was the daughter of Richard and Margaret, for under 18th February 1748 she was baptised together with a twin brother, Joseph, but the latter died the following year.

The William Ames referred to as her uncle was the toymaker and it appears that he became feeble-minded and he was put into care—possibly with Mr. Proud. He died in 1784.

GREEN

THERE were people of this name in Bilston long before the 18th century. In Elizabeth's reign an Edward Green and a John Green were renting a small piece of land; Edward Green was bailiff of Stowheath Manor in 1601.[19] In the 1699 Manor Chief Rent Roll,[20] a William Green, ' gent. ', and a John Green, are both shown as not ' New-comers ' and property owners.

However, Ames's first register of 1695 lists the above John, Ann, his wife and children, John and Richard; William would appear to have been living elsewhere. Members of the Green family may have come to Bilston from Walsall for a Joseph Green was in Bilston as a bucklemaker by 1716. He would appear to have been maried elsewhere but his sons, George (1716) and Richard (1718) were born here and a Thomas Green ' from Walsall ' was buried in 1749 in Bilston and in the same year John Green, ' parish of Walsall ', married Margaret Read at Wolverhampton. In the Pearson and Rollason Directory of 1781, there are eight men named Green in the list of Walsall tradesmen and seven were bucklemakers; to add to the problem the same directory has a John Green, steelbucklemaker, in Wolverhampton.

John Green married Mary Dovey at Wolverhampton in 1709,

both being domiciled in Bilston. Both of his sons, John and Richard became bucklemakers, but John added toymaking to his work, for in 1742 he took Richard Newton as an apprentice, and in 1744 Joshua Smith, thus proving that he was successfully established, and, no doubt, the familiar family associations helped; for instance in 1744 we find that John Green, together with Dovey Hawksford and Matthew Birch, paid £26.10s.0d. for three seats in the new gallery of the church. Moreover Esther Dovey, a relative of Dovey Hawksford, at one time was living in a house owned by John Green. He and William Homer the enameller were the collectors of the Land Tax for the year 1738 and presented these accounts and those of the Overseers in 1739.

John outlived his brother Richard for the latter's widow, Anne, herself died in 1747. But John had a son christened John, born in 1757 and this is the man who became the bucklemaker and enameller of the directories of 1770 and 1781. He had obviously extended the family business, for as early as 1762 he is described as a boxmaker and he took Edward Marson as an apprentice. He is also described as a boxmaker in the will of his brother Edward, who was a bucklemaker, in 1753. Edward's estate was sworn as less than £20 and most of it went to John. In Bailey's 'British Directory' of 1784 he is called an enameller.

It is difficult to assess how successful John Green was. The Land Survey of 1771 shows him having two small pieces totalling about five acres and there is a reference in the will of Benjamin Bickley's third wife (Mary Birch), in 1780, to 'two guineas for mourning to John Green of Bilston, enameller'. Also a beneficiary was William Green, victualler, who might well have had some association with John's and the Bickley's enamelling enterprises. He does not appear to have been prominent in the town's affairs, though he was Constable in 1738, and his business may have been a small one, others looking after his trading interest; it is possible that he made gilt-metal mounts, some of which may have been used by family associates.

The Greens lived in a good-sized, half-timbered house in High Street. This had been the old Manor or Court House of Stowheath[21] and it is today the oldest house in Bilston. It is now called the Greyhound Inn and the brewery which owns it has taken great care to maintain its character. One wing only remains now, indicative of the size of the original building which, before Green, had been the home of the well-to-do Mollesley family. The date 1458 is found on a beam in one of the upper rooms.

By 1827, according to Smart's 'Wolverhampton Directory', Robert Reeve was in possession of the Old Greyhound Inn. Price, in his 'Historical Account of Bilston', has, on page 25, a foot-note about a house near the church later occupied by the famed John Etheridge. He states that it was sold (1750) by Sir Richard Wrottesley to John Green whose representatives sold it to the ancestor of Mr. Etheridge. Green did not live there himself.

As in the case of the Smiths previously mentioned, there were a number of Greens in Bilston, for instance from 1750-1760 we find a Perry, John, Thomas, Joseph and William all named as fathers in the Baptisms Register, while the deaths include a Thomas, from Walsall, in 1749, an Edward in 1753 and a Richard in 1756—not children.

Another Green, Thomas, owned some 30 acres according to the 1770 Levy Books, but it is the John Greens whom we associate with the enamel trade in Bilston.

KNOWLES

THIS family was of humble origin and in the 1695 Parish Register there was, in Bilston, a Richard Knowles, Ann, his wife and a son William; another son, Richard, appears to have been born later. The name is not found in the 1699 Chief Rent Roll and it does not appear in the church account of officers, pew holders, and others, but a Richard Knowles, noted above, in 1692 was paid 4d. 'for removing ye bricks into ye chapel' while in 1694 Ann Knowles was paid 2s.9d. 'for dressing and sweeping ye Chapel', probably in preparation for a church festival.

A William Knowles married Joan Perry in 1702; if this was the above William he married young and among his children was another William, born in 1715. They became bucklemakers and two sons were born to the younger William, Thomas, in 1739 and John, in 1741. In 1746 he took as an apprentice Richard Knowles, probably his nephew, for his brother Richard had a son Richard in 1733, by his wife Elizabeth Hanson; this son had died young, for a second was christened Richard, in 1736. He had married Elizabeth Hanson in 1729 from a family probably engaged in similar work. This indenture describes William as a toymaker—a development we have seen previously. In 1733 he was living in a house in Bilston belonging to Sir Richard Wrottesley, of an ancient Staffordshire family; Sir Richard was in Holy Orders and in 1756 officiated at the marriage of his sister at Tettenhall.

Like many parents of the time, William and his wife Mary lost several children in infancy; one daughter was christened Isaac (sic) in 1748, but she died two years later and a son Joseph did not survive any longer. However another Joseph Knowles was apprenticed to John Castey, toymaker, in 1747; probably not a Bilston boy.

This family seems to present another example of the changes from bucklemaker to toymaker and then enameller. In 1763 Richard Knowles, described as a toymaker, took Thomas Johns as an apprentice, but a few years later the man we find called an enameller is Thomas Knowles—an enamelled boxmaker. This was, one assumes, the son of William, the bucklemaker and who had been born in 1739. However, the elder William Knowles had had a son christened Thomas in 1719 and on his early death had passed the same christian name to another child in 1722. Thomas Knowles married Elizabeth Stokes in 1752, but an early death removed several of his young sons.

Perhaps Thomas and Richard had worked in close co-operation but not in a big way. Even at the time of his appearance in the directory, Thomas did not appear to own or rent any land. It could be that the original workshop was attached to the house his father had rented from Wrottesley, but John Freeman says the house of Thomas Knowles, a descendant of Thomas, was near the old Cock Inn, which was situated at the junction of Willenhall Road and Darlaston Lane, and that it had been occupied by the family for 120 years. This site would be about the same distance —in the opposite direction—from the town centre as Bickley's Ettingshall Lodge, but close to the Bickley's Meynell House.

As no Knowles occurs in the 1781 directory it is likely that this small firm turned to other types of work, and Freeman states that the business had changed from the declining chape manuafcture

73

to tin-plate working. A certain John Knowles was apprenticed to John Dowler in 1771 to learn the trade of bucklemaker. He was probably the son born to Richard Knowles in 1765 and Thomas in 1763. Thomas himself died in 1778. However, there could have been other Knowles men working in Bilston and probably marrying there; a George (1741), John (1754), Matthew (1756), George (1757), Thomas (1759), Thomas (1768), and a number of others, but the Wolverhampton register does not include Bilston residents so that one cannot be certain in all cases. Nevertheless, with reference to bonds in the Parish Register regarding paternity cases, a William and Richard Knowles had to find £40 between them in July 1763.

This was not the first misdemeanour, for a Thomas and William in 1749 and a Richard and Thomas in 1760 had been charged a similar penalty for the same offence. Thomas Knowles is described as a tin-plate worker of Cold Lanes in the Commercial Directory for 1818-19-20 and this would appear to be the man Freeman was writing about. He could not be the victualler who died in 1812. The Chapel Warden's Levies for 1818 show him charged £2 for his house, the levy being two payments of 6d. in the pound.

BRETT

EGAN Mew names James Brett as an enameller in Bilston and John Freeman in his ' Bilston Almanac Sketches '[22] writes as follows:—' On the right side of Bridge Street stood a notable group of three storied houses in one of which lived the artist James Brett, one of the fathers of the Bilston enamel trade '. He also claims that he worked at the trade from 1760 to 1779.[23]

There were no Bretts in the town when Ames compiled his register in 1695 and no births or deaths recorded up to 1730, nor do we find the name in the earlier Apprentice Lists. There were, however, Bretts in neighbouring Wolverhampton, for William Brett served as a churchwarden there in 1708 and 1709 and a Thomas Brett in 1720 and 1721; the Wolverhampton Register records a James Brett marrying Dorothy Lees of Pattingham, in 1731.

From the several families named Brett in Wolverhampton[24]

some moved to Bilston in the 1735-36 period for Isaac Brett, John and Charles appear to have been married and settled here, for baptisms of children of the three are recorded between 1737 and 1739. Bretts buried at Bilston include Samuel (1764) Thomas (1767) and Isaac (1774) and Charles's will describes him as of Bilston (1762). A Samuel Brett was Constable in nearby Willenhall in 1746 and, in Bilston, a daughter of William Brett was christened Rebecca in 1747. He is described as 'from Willenhall' and he had a son Joseph born in 1759. Another Brett—Thomas —had three sons—William, Benjamin and Thomas; he died in 1767. The Wolverhampton Bretts were bucklemakers and the Birmingham Directory for 1767 gives Benjamin Brett as a steel bucklemaker, while the 1770 list has Henry, George, John, Richard and Thomas all as metal bucklemakers. The 1781 Directory has Richard a bucklemaker, Benjamin a steel bucklemaker, and Henry and Thomas were still engaged in the same trade.

Benjamin Brett married Sarah Gascoin in 1738 and was a bucklemaker and toymaker; he had two sons, George and Benjamin. He died in 1766 and it could be his son George who is referred to in Mr. Starkie Gardener's book 'Some Minor Arts' as setting up a rival establishment to Battersea about 1750. Egan Mew does not support this, but William Chaffers in his 'Marks and Monograms on Pottery and Porcelain' published in 1876 names George Brett as an enameller. He also claims that he was the enameller from whose factory came the large collection of pieces in the later Bickley family's possession. This is refuted by Bernard and Therle Hughes in 'English Painted Enamels' who had facts given to them personally suggesting a different version for the origin of the pieces.

Was there a George Brett who worked as an enameller? Certainly a George married, in 1742, a girl named Esther Pain who did not survive very long, for he married Phoebe Hammersley in 1746. Did Chaffers make a mistake over the christian name and really mean James? James married Catharine Brett, perhaps a cousin, in 1744. Perhaps he did not, for first if George was the son of the Wolverhampton bucklemaker, Benjamin, and secondly if he was brother of the younger Benjamin who left a house in Bilston Street, Wolverhampton, to him at his death— and here it should be noted that most of the Brett workshops were situated in this part of Wolverhampton and it is nearest to Bilston—and if thirdly George was either at Bilston or Bilston Street then it is not beyond the bounds of reason to suppose he knew something about enamelling.

The catalogue of the Schreiber Collection 1884 presented to the South Kensington Museum contained the following:[25] 'At Bilston enamelling on copper was practised by George Brett and other artists, the best work having been produced about 1760-1770'. Seven pieces were listed, all printed in black and were of Admiral Rodney, Capt. Farmer, 1779, Dr. Franklin, George Washington, General Reed of America 1778, H.M.S. Vanguard 1798, and Gloucester Cathedral.

Neither George nor James appears in the 1770 or 1781 directory. Their names are also missing from the 1771 Land Register, so it is probable that neither achieved much distinction; however they may have left the town. James was apparently in Bilston in the 1760's when two children were christened there, but neither George nor James was buried in Bilston.

HANSON

ANOTHER enameller mentioned by Freeman is Samuel Hanson.[26] He lived in a substantial house on Swan Bank in Bilston, a house which still stands. At one time it was occupied by the Birmingham District Bank[27] and it is still used for banking purposes. Freeman states that Hanson 'followed the calling with success for many years'. In 1771 he held two plots of land, one of which is described as 'Pipe's Meadow' and the house and workshop would be on this site, the name still being in use today. His is another name not found in the directories, but he may have had family connections with the John Hanson who is called a box-painter in 1756, based at Wolverhampton. There were Hansons there at the beginning of the century—Richard married in 1707, John 1715 and George in 1726. Later we find a William married in 1732 and Thomas in 1735.

Probably related to these was the Richard Hanson who married Elizabeth Perry at Bilston, 28th June 1745. If she were the widow of Joseph Perry the elder, toymaker, we can see a possible connection with the Perry enamelling business. The only

Hanson who appears in the register in the next twenty or so years is a Benjamin Hanson, who did not have a son Samuel; yet, on the other hand, John Hanson was a prominent citizen in Bilston at the time as the Vestry Book shows:—

In 1762 the elected Overseers of the Poor include John Hanson, gent. and his signature appears on the appointment of a 'Surgeon and Apothecary for the Workhouse' in the same year. John Hanson, in 1762, was also appointed as one of the ten 'Surveyors of the Highways' so that he would appear to be the man concerned, as one of the requirements of the office was a certain financial standing. The 1771 Land Survey only gives the surname Hanson. Was Samuel Hanson, the son of John, who had perhaps moved to Bilston to the centre of the enamelling trade and then set up his own workshop? The 1781 Directory has 'Hanson and Jacks—merchants and japanners'.

Sam. Hanson subscribed five guineas to the Defence of the Nation Appeal in 1798. His name and signature occur frequently in the Vestry Book 1791-1814, for instance, in the affairs of the Overseers, and in 1802 he served on the committee elected to examine the accounts. He died intestate, letters of administration being granted to his widow, Elizabeth, 31st March 1806 and sworn at under £450. But he is called a japanner here, so that if Freeman is correct, he would appear to have combined the two trades.

HOO FOSTER

THE very first entry in Ames' Register of 1695 was John Hoo, widower, and it was followed by Mrs. Joan Hoo, widow, and then the names of their three servants, but no children. John Hoo owned the only three 'habitations' in that part of Bilston called Bradley, one being Bradley Hall where he lived,[28] and he was one of the fifteen customary tenants who, in turn, acted as bailiff.

In one document he is also referred to as Sergeant-at-law. In 1710 he purchased the neighbouring manor of Wednesbury[29] and he acquired the manor of Great Barr through his marriage.

When Queen Anne granted Wednesbury a charter for the holding of a market, Hoo is described as 'barrister-at-law-'. He died in 1719 at Sergeants Inn, London, and was buried in St. Peter's Collegiate Church, Wolverhampton.[30]

His family had been Lords of the Manor of Bradley for many years; at the Herald's Visitation of 1663-64, John Hoo had his arms recorded and his crest, granted in 1614, confirmed.

Dr. Plot mentions in his notes on Bilston,[31] that at Bilston quarry, there was obtained a very hard stone, very suitable for cisterns and troughs, and that Mr. Hoo ' got here one eight yards long and not more than one inch variance in the whole length '!

John Hoo's heir, also John, of Barr, West Bromwich, succeeded to the estate and this eventually passed to the second nephew Thomas. In the 1770 list, Thomas appears as one of the principal landowners, having about 208 acres, mainly in the Bradley area. Price says that the celebrated John Wilkinson first worked for Hoo at his Bradley mines in 1756, when he was 27 years of age.[32] Wilkinson however, had soon established his own works in the same area. Thomas prospered from the land and mines he owned and in 1772 he was appointed High Sheriff. The family home must have been an imposing building for the Hearth Tax Returns for 1673 gives 12 to be paid for. Thomas Hoo died in 1791.

We do not associate the Hoo family directly with the enamel trade, but now turn to Foster. Freeman refers to a Mr. Foster, ' the banker of Foster's Fold '. The concern with banking of the Fosters appears to have continued into the next century, for White's Directory of 1834 mentions John Foster, banker, Lich-field Street; this was in the centre of the town. He was one of the committee concerned with the 1832 Cholera Appeal.

There was a Richard Foster earlier in Bilston, who had a son named Richard, but the possible sequence of events is that some wealthy outsider settled in Bilston and one of the family married a girl from the Hoo family and took the additional name of Hoo. At some time an enamelling business was established, probably later than some of the others in Bilston, in the area of Foster's Fold, to the western end of the main street. The Commercial Directory of 1818 records Thomas Hoo Foster as an enameller in High Street; he could, of course, have been the proprietor of the enamelling business rather than an actual enameller, or even acquired the factory through the marriage. The ' Parson and Bradshaw Directory ' of 1818 calls him an ' enameller in general '.

There was a Thomas Foster who married Ann Perry, in September 1760, and there is a possible connection with the Perry enamellers here, but the Marriage Register does not indicate the couples or individuals from Bilston at this period. This is a disadvantage, for we find another Thomas Foster marrying in 1762 and another Foster-Perry marriage took place in 1769, this time of Simon and Mary. One of the Thomas Fosters would be the man who in 1770 claimed the estate of his father Samuel, since his mother had died intestate. It was sworn at under £20.

REFERENCES
[1] G. B. Hughes, 'Collecting Antiques', pp. 29, 72.
[2] Aris' Gazette.
[3] P. 33. Also S.R.S., 1915, p. 391, Roman Catholic Landowners in 1648.
[4] J. Freeman, 'Wesleyan Methodism in Bilston', p. 6 states that another branch of the family lived in an old half-timbered house on the site of the Public Baths. Also see Price, pp. 58-59.
[5] Lawley, p. 33.
[6] Pp. 149-153.
[7] G. Mander, Apprenticeship Transcripts (see p.   ).
[8] Price, pp. 72-75.
[9] G. Mander, Preface to 1925 Exhibition Catalogue.
[10] Price, p. 120.
[11] Price, p. 54.
[12] Apprentice Lists. See p.   .
[13] P. 12.
[14] P. 6.
[15] Price, p. 83.
[16] Ibid., p. 93.
[17] W.S.L., Hand Morgan Collection.
[18] Parish Register, p. 115.
[19] S.R.S., 1923, pp. 62-64. Richard Green exempt from Hearth Tax 1666
[20] Price, p. 31.
[21] Price, p. 59. It may have been merely the Court House.
[22] Chapter 3, 1908, p. 11.
[23] Ibid., p. 23.
[24] N. W. Tildesley, M.S.S., 'The Church Wardens of Wolverhampton gives two Bretts 1708-9 and 1720-21.
[25] B. Racksham, 'Cat. of Schreiber Collection, Vol. III, p. 26-72. W. Chaffers, 'Marks and Monograms on Pottery and Porcelain', 3rd edition, p. 979.
[26] 'Bilston Almanack Sketches', 1908, p. 23.
[27] Ibid., 1910, p. 35.
[28] S.R.S., 1923 Hearth Tax Returns 1666, p. 62-64. Hoo paid for twelve chimneys.
[29] Lawley, p. 138.
[30] Parish Register, p. 68.
[31] Dr. Robert Plot, 'The Natural History of Staffordshire', 1686.
[32] 'The Story of Bilston', p. 20.

8

BOX PAINTERS

THE descriptions of crafts and trades distinguished between box maker and box painter. The artist who learned how to apply enamel colours to the copper base would be judged and rewarded by the quality of the final product after the firings. While it is conceivable that a first class box painter could be called in and commissioned to carry out a particular order by a box maker or toy maker, it is also feasible to conclude that a box painter worked in a shop and supervised the firings; in other words he was the enameller, especially in a small workshop, and this could be his own business.

The box painters were remarkably skilled in the art of applying small quantities of enamel, with fine brushes, to the plain enamel base on the metal surface. If one thinks of a miniature head-and-shoulder portrait of some two or three inches, or the number of delicate strokes required on a rustic scene, landscape of group of figures with background, then one realises the skill, concentration and patience required of the enamel painter. This is true whether he was painting an individual piece or a transfer print. Moreover, he needed to know about the preparation and composition of his enamel powders and their behaviour under different firing conditions.

We have to wait until the first half of the eighteenth century had almost passed before we find, as noted earlier, the first attempts at box painting in Bilston; subsequently we get the names of apprentices. The premiums demanded were high, beyond the reach of ordinary working-class people, and some degree of innate artistic ability was required. It was, naturally, the type of delicate work at which a girl could succeed, and it must be borne in mind that a trained painter in enamelling could, without great difficulty, switch over to painting japanned work.

THOMAS BAYLISS

ONE of the first men to be designated 'box painter' was Thomas Bayliss. Reference has already been made to him as probably working for Richard Ames in his workshop at Priestfields. There is no reference to a family named Bayliss during the first thirty years of the century, so that Thomas may have had some early training elsewhere before joining Ames, perhaps in Birmingham or Darlaston, where some of this name are found. In any event he must have been a competent workman by 1753 when he is described as a box painter; in 1758 he took Hannah Taylor as an apprentice. It is not known whether he continued in Bilston, perhaps at Priestfields, or whether he moved to another centre such as Wednesbury or Birmingham; he is not recorded as owning or renting any land in 1771.

Although there was no family of the name of Bayliss when the curate came to Bilston in 1684 there was a William and his wife, named as Baylies, by 1708, when a son, also William, was baptised, followed by another William (1711), Joseph (1713) and George (1716). William Baylies is described as a bricklayer in 1719 and as a mason when he was buried in 1728.

There follows a gap with no births recorded until 1738. In that year, a son William was born to George and Mary Bayliss in Bilston and in 1740 they had a son Thomas who could have been the boy who went to Ames; we do not know his father's occupation. There are two interesting weddings recorded at Wolverhampton. First that of Thomas Bayliss to Elizabeth Davis in 1718, and secondly that of Thomas Bayliss and Elizabeth Done in 1723; the second Thomas is not recorded as bachelor or widower. Here it seems we may have the father of the box painter, for since Thomas the painter was with Ames in the 1750s he could not be the Thomas Baylies born to the Thomas and Catharine in 1747 and baptised at Bilston. The conclusion then appears to be that, if he were not George's son, the apprentice made the short journey from Wolverhampton to Priestfield. When he had completed his indenture he settled in Bilston, conceivably at Priestfield.

This was almost certainly in 1758, or a little earlier, for he was in business himself in that year and able to take Hannah

81

Taylor as an apprentice, soon, one would imagine, to paint such things as the sides of enamelled boxes before going on to more precise work on the lids and painting japanned goods. It may be that he did not stay in Bilston as there is no record of him marrying, but, of course, he may have remained a bachelor; the latter explanation might account for the fact that a Thomas Bayliss died in Bilston in 1799. It is probable that there was a separate and distinct family with no connection with the box painter for the name and spelling occur again in a 1765 marriage entry at Wolverhampton close to a 'Baylis' spelling in 1754. The 'Bailies' form appears in three burials recorded between 1748 and 1772 in the Bilston register.

PENELOPE CARLESS

A N example of a girl being described as a box painter is Penelope Carless, who in June 1762 took Edward Perry as an apprentice; he was the son of Joseph Perry, toymaker, already mentioned, and was later associated with the family enamelling business. The Carless family was descended from the gallant Colonel Carless who was with Charles II in the oak tree at Boscobel and for whom a memorial tablet was erected in nearby Brewood Church. There is no record of a Carless family in the 1695 register, nor do we find one among the many bucklemakers, chapers, toymakers and others of the 1700-1730 period. They came to Bilston from Birmingham it would appear, Lawley thinks from Harborne,[1] a Birmingham suburb, and with sufficient funds to set up in business.

The Revd. Edward Best recorded the following baptism in 1752. 'Carless Thos. s. of Edward, gent., of ye family of the Carless', late of Corbyn's Hall, and Elizabeth his wife who was the eldest daughter of Thomas Tomkys of Nechells Esq. The Tomkys family were gentry of long standing of Bilston. This child died in infancy and the curate usually referred to his father as 'gent.', as occurs in the baptismal entry for a second son, William in 1753.

With spelling not always reliable at the time, there is some difficulty over reference to both 'Carless' and 'Careless'; however the Carless family was soon established in Bilston for we find the following in the list of Chapel Wardens:—

1753   Edward Carless and Thomas Pratchett (taking over from
       Isaac Beckett)
1754   Richard Carless and Thomas Pratchett
1755   Richard Carless and Thomas Pratchett

The interesting point is that Edward and Richard were brothers and Pratchett married their sister, Elizabeth 'eldest daughter of Joseph Careless'. A daughter of 'Thomas gent. and Elizabeth Pratchett' was christened Mary on April 2nd 1758. Thomas died in 1758 and again reference is made in the register to the fact that he married Elizabeth Carless, eldest daughter of the late Joseph of Corbyn's Hall in the Co. of Staffs.

She survived a further twenty five years. That the three men were associated in business is obvious and since Edward was a japanner they may have done enamelling also; however Richard married a Penelope Yorke, our box painter, so it is fairly conclusive that enamel work was done at an early date in Bilston, for both Edward and Richard were dead by 1755.

There is a tablet in Saint Leonard's Church, Bilston, inscribed as follows: ' Richard, son of Joseph Carless of Corbyn's Hall, died 20th May 1755 aged 40 and was buried near this place '. There is a coat-of-arms of Colonel Carless. Under 23rd May 1755, the Revd. Best wrote ' Richard Carless gent., was Chapel Warden in the present year, brother of the late Mr. Edward Carless who died in his Chapel Wardenship '. According to Best he met with a terrible accident[2]; he wrote ' He went into the store room to examine a vessel of Spirit Varnish heating in a stove '. It took fire and he was terribly burnt and he died eleven days later; one can imagine his agony. He was in his twenty-eighth year. Best calls him ' my near neighbour and acquaintance ' and devotes many lines to his praise.

He also has another interesting entry for the same year: ' On 15th April James Pratchett, Clerk, Curate of Adderley in Shropshire and Mrs. Mary Carless of Bilston, daughter of ye late Joseph Carless of Corbyn's Hall Esq. were married by me in Wolverhampton Church under licence from Mr. Craddock '. This was another bond between the two families.

Since Penelope Carless was a widow in 1755 and took an apprentice box painter in 1762, it seems that she carried on the

83

business, possibly doing less practical work and more supervising and managing. Her own training took place outside Bilston, one would suppose from the dates known, but she was obviously a competent artist. Gerald Mander relates that she left, as a bequest, a remarkable enamelled plaque showing, in gay colouring and amid a festooned border, a representation of the Carless armorial bearings. She may have painted it and perhaps her husband made and fired it; on the other hand she may have done the work herself during her widowhood.

It is not known what happened to the workshop; Penelope may have sold it and eventually left Bilston, as did others of the family, for no one of the name Carless owned or rented any land in 1771. There were other Carless (or Careless) people in Bilston including another Edward and Joseph, but there is no evidence to connect them with the 'gentry'. A Richard Careless suffered the tragic loss of his wife Mary and daughter Mary in the space of a few months in 1762.

JOHN SIMMONS

THE next important boxpainter is John Simmons who came to Bilston in 1741 to be apprenticed to Dovey Hawksford who, we have seen, had been described as a toymaker but, on this occasion was recorded as a chapman. There was no family of the name in the town but his parents had been able to afford a reasonable standard of education for him and to pay the not inconsiderable premium demanded.

During his time with Hawksford he would see enamelling introduced. The painting aspect of the work seems to have appealed to him and, no doubt, he had opportunities to try his hand, for later on he called himself a box painter. When Hawksford died in 1749, Simmons probably felt capable of carrying on alone and he settled in the town, following the Carless brothers in the office of Church Warden, and serving in that capacity from 1756 to 1762 as the elected representative of the parishioners, not as the curate's nominee. Another public office he filled was the important one of Constable in 1767.

In 1758, Simmons accepted Philadelphia Parkes an an apprentice and is here described as a toymaker, so it is possible that he had a workshop where the various types of 'toys' were made, painted, and fired and finished ready for sale. He also turned his attention to japanning where his skill as a painter could be used to advantage. In the 1770 directory published by George Smart at Walsall, John Simmons is described as a japanner and in Bailey's 'Western and Midland Directory for 1783' we find, 'John Simmons and Son, japanners'. This would be his son John, born to his wife Mary, in 1756, their only child to survive.

If John Simmons came to Bilston in 1741 as an apprentice, he could scarcely be the same man as the John Simmons whose wife, Mary, bore a son John in 1749, who died within a few months, a daughter Mary in 1750, Samuel in 1754 and Sarah in 1752. Our John Simmons and his wife, also Mary, would appear to be the parents of a son Joseph who died in infancy, in 1763, and two daughters; the burial entry for Elizabeth, one of the daughters, describes her father as 'gent.'. Difficulty in distinguishing the family is also seen in the fact that the Wolverhampton Marriage Register has another John and Mary Simmons for the year 1773, but since both of these made their sign, this is obviously another pair, for our John Simmons signed his name in beautiful handwriting in the Parish Register.

With a prosperous business and a son to help, John seems to have sought a change from the confines of the workshop; he acted as chapman for his own wares and probably those of other manufacturers in the town, being so designated in the Vestry Minutes of September 22nd 1758.

Before leaving the box painters, mention should be made of some others who, even if they did not live in Bilston itself, were near enough to do such work for their own productions or else on behalf of the enamellers in Bilston since they were less than half an hour's walking distance of their premises. John Hanson has already been referred to in connection with Samuel Hanson. He took an apprentice to learn box painting in 1756 and it is possible that he was more concerned with japan work as there is no evidence of any enamelling establishment in Wolverhampton. There were many bucklemakers, including mainly steel bucklemakers, in the town and some japanners, so that Hanson, the boxpainter, could well have done work for Bilston box and toy makers.

Much the same may be said of William Cox who is listed as a box painter (1756) and painter (1762-63) in the Register of Apprentices. If he is the same William Cox who went to Richard Ames in 1743 at Priestfields then he could have been experienced in both enamelling and japanning work, with his own workshop, or painting for other men in Wolverhampton or Bilston. A William Cox married Mary Till at Wolverhampton in 1753 and a William Cox, bachelor, married Elizabeth Ravens there in 1757. Depending on the age of Cox when he went to Ames one of these is our man.

Another Cox, who could have been related to the above, was Edward Cox of Sedgley. The buildings of this parish would be centred on the Bull Ring and parish church, a few miles only from Bilston, but in part the boundary was adjacent to that of Bilston, and for some length of it the Bilston Brook was the dividing line. This makes it possible for Cox to have been quite close to the Bilston workshops; even if he worked in the heart of Sedgley he would be fully conversant with what was going on in Bilston.

Also of interest in this connection is that an Edward Cox of Bilston married Jemima Newton of Sedgley in 1746. The Apprentices Register shows him as taking a young man in 1755 as a box painter, another in 1759 as a snuff-box maker and a third in 1760 as a box painter. References to both 'box maker' and 'painter' points to Cox having his own workshop and completing the processes with firing the boxes; he may have specialised in manufacturing.

———

REFERENCES
[1] Lawley, p. 119.
[2] 19th January 1754.

9

THE ENGRAVERS

THE work of engravers received a boost when the art of transfer printing was discovered and mastered. There is some doubt as to who first made transfer prints on enamel but the technique was practised in Bilston some time after 1756 followin its successful use in Battersea and Liverpool. Engraved plates may have been purchased when the York House factory closed in 1756; a redundant employee from there may have moved to South Staffordshire or a skilled craftsman could have set up a 'shop' in Bilston.

As in the case of the enamel painters the abilities of the engravers varied; in addition to an artistic sense, great patience and skill was necessary in using the tools to cut the numerous lines on the copper plate. It was so easy to ruin carefully executed work with, for example, the slip of a scriber. The engraver could work from his own ideas and choose his own subjects; he could work to the requirements of a particular customer or he could use and adapt to his own purpose the work of artists, either from an individual picture or book of illustrations and designs. In the Artists 'Vade Mecum', advertised by Robert Sayer in 1762,[1] books of drawing for sale are advertised and 146 books on different subjects are noted at one shilling and six pence each, eight different books of views of villages and other scenes near London at six pence each, and 18 different books of views of Holland at six pence each. In the case of a national event of rejoicing or a catastrophe he could produce his engraved plate; some enameller, japanner or potter would be only too ready to purchase it and produce dozens of items for sale to eager customers. On the other hand he could well have the facilities to do the work himself.

The engravings produced covered a wide range, from the

highly artistic and beautiful picture to a simple little design on a patch box with its crude, small central drawing such as of an urn surrounded by a love motto or political slogan. What use was made of the engraved plate was not necessarily the concern of the engraver, and he need not be present at the subsequent transfer-printing and enamelling; in other words he was not obliged to be resident in Bilston, and chapmen, for example, could make his work known and available. At the same time it must be realised that an engraver could use his plates, do the transfer printing and paint and fire the pieces in his own workshop or in that of a relative or friend. In any case he would probably make the actual transfer sheets himself, or supervise their production, for each would need to be checked for possible 'touching up' to be done where the inked outline had not taken completely.

John Vardon was such an artist in Bilston. It has been supposed that he was the son of the Revd. William Vardon, rector at neighbouring Darlaston. The rector was in Bilston in February 1725, on a Sunday, to attest the public penance of a girl because Ames was indisposed. The Revd. Vardon died in 1741 and there is no record of a son of his, named John, being baptised there. Nevertheless John Vardon was living in Bilston in 1753, for in April of that year a daughter, Mary, was christened, the child of John and Esther Vardon. He appears to have been married elsewhere than at Wolverhampton or Bilston, perhaps Darlaston. Other children born later were also baptized at Saint Leonard's and, when John died in 1792, he had spent some forty years in Bilston. The names of both John and his wife are entered in the Register of Burials; Esther died in 1786. In the 1770 and 1781 directories he is described as an engraver and box-painter.

Mr. Eric Benton, in a paper read to the English Ceramic Circle, states that there was a John Vardon working in a small way as a toymaker in Birmingham in 1745. In this year he took an apprentice. Unfortunately there is a gap in the Apprentices List for Bilston for the period 1745-1750 and we cannot say definitely where John served his apprenticeship. He could have been a relative of the Birmingham man, but as he was married about 1751, he had obviously completed his apprenticeship before that date. Whatever form that took it probably had little to do with engraving and his early work in Bilston would not be as an engraver.

When transfer-printing became the 'new thing' in Bilston his artistic leanings may have led him to preparing plates, with limited success, but his skill would improve through practice and experiment. His marriage gave him contacts with some of the leading enamellers in the town and there was plenty of work for him both as an engraver and box painter. He probably did work for the Becketts or Bickleys or both, at different times.

With regard to actual examples of Vardon's work, it is difficult to be certain as there are no distinguishing marks or 'clues'. He did not achieve the fine artistic standards of people like Robert Hancock. Gerald Mander, among others, made a close study of the work of Vardon's period and some engravings which may have been his include:—

Captain Farmer, who died in 1779.
Prince William Henry (afterwards William IV) who joined the Navy in 1779.
General Clinton who was prominent in the American War of Independence, 1780.
Lord Cornwallis, 1781.
Admiral Rodney, who won a victory in 1780.

Such plates served to provide the portrait for enamelled oval plaques to be hung, and the transfer could be reduced in size for such things as box lids or brooches. The type of engravings Vardon would work on normally would include rustic scenes, sporting subjects and 'views' for souvenir boxes, to meet the huge demand from places like Cheltenham, Bath, and other towns.

Mander suggested that Bilston enamels decorated with transfer engravings in black and coloured inks, carefully drawn and well finished, may be his work, as also examples showing people with broad faces. The excellent plates made by Robert Hancock would be known to Vardon and possibly he copied from them but with less proficiency. There are strong reasons for believing that plates engraved by Robert Hancock were known and used in Bilston though he himself was never resident there. He was born in the pottery district of Staffordshire about 1730 and he was apprenticed to George Anderton, a Birmingham engraver, for a fee of thirty pounds, which suggests that he went to a good master.[2] This was in 1746, and on completing his apprenticeship about 1753, he went to London and probably after a brief period at the Bow porcelain factory he moved to Battersea[3] where he came under the influence of men like Ravenet, the first class French designer and engraver, Boitard, another French artist, and John Brooks, the Irishman. Boitard may not have been employed at Battersea but have done free-lance work.[4]

Cyril Cook in ' Apollo ', 1953, says there is no proof that Boitard was at York House, but his name occurs, with Ravenet's, in Len's foreword to the ' Drawing Book ' of 1751. Hancock made use of some of his designs. A few snuff boxes and plaques bear Boitard's name as ' sculp ' or designer. It was John Brooks who introduced the technique of transfer printing to York House. In all probability he had experimented with the process previously in Birmingham.[5] It was Hancock's good fortune to be associated with these talented experts while still a young man and he learned much from them and was influenced by their artistic ability and style.

When the Battersea factory was closed in 1756, Hancock moved to the Worcester Porcelain Works, where his ability as an engraver was quickly recognised; in 1772 he became a partner in the firm. Cyril Cook states that Hancock worked at the Bow porcelain factory for a time, possibly as early as 1755.[6] He could have produced plates for use there and learnt something of the processes involved, which knowledge would have been useful when he moved to Worcester. His engravings were finely and delicately lined and his transfers were skilfully applied to the plates and other surfaces. Some of his work on porcelain can be identified and it is highly prized by collectors; the initials R.H. are a guide, but unfortunately they are also those of another prominent worker at Worcester at the time. Following internal disputes at the factory, Hancock left in 1775. He sold his share in the business, one sixth, for nine hundred pounds and moved to the Caughley porcelain works; then he had the misfortune to lose his savings in a bank failure. Hancock probably became rather disillusioned with the porcelain industry and turned to other fields where engraved plates were in great demand.

Neither Worcester nor Caughley were too distant for Hancock's work not to be known in the South Staffordshire area, nor for him to be unaware of the opportunities open to a talented engraver. It was not necessary for a ' free-lance ' engraver to be confined to work in one particular place, and in 1770, for instance, he, with the assistance of two other young artists, prepared the dozen or so plates for a book from the press of Thomas Smith in Wolverhampton. In 1780 he was at Oldbury,[7] and the following year at Tipton, both places near to Bilston and Wednesbury, not to mention Birmingham, where there was an increasing demand for the work of engravers. Hackwood, in his ' Oldbury and Round About ', states that Hancock devoted himself at Oldbury to engraving in mezzotint.

Cyril Cook in his ' Life and Work of Robert Hancock '[8] says that Hancock, at this time, was again concerned with the actual printing of enamels and that ' there are quite a number of specimens which, in 1924, were thought to have been printed in the neighbourhood of Bilston . . . from copper plates which, it is believed, he took with him when he left Worcester '. This seems perfectly feasible considering his experience at Battersea.

In 1784 the engraver was resident in Birmingham and, among other work, he supplied plates for the firm of Pearson and Rollason, his chief interest then being in portrait engraving. This firm produced an illustrated edition of the Bible in 1788, thirty five of the plates were signed by Hancock. No doubt his talents and services were used by other Birmingham firms such as japanners and enamellers. Hancock also engraved the plate for Thomas Hanson's ' Plan of Birmingham ' in 1785, shown in Pye's ' Birmingham directory for 1791 '.

After his experience at Worcester, it seems logical to deduce that his success in this field would lead to some contact with the pottery works he had known in North Staffordshire, even if only to sell engraved plates. Hackwood mentions that engraved plates were found at that other famous factory in Shropshire, Coalport, which were the work of Hancock. His last move was to Bristol[9] and then, being more advanced in years, his chief interest was in producing portraits in pencil and crayon. He exhibited two pictures at the Royal Academy in 1805 and took a keen interest in the work of his son Robert, himself an artist and painter of miniatures, to whom he left his collection of paintings, prints, and other items when he died in 1817. Another son, Thomas, was working in Birmingham as an engraver up to the end of the century and was described as such in his father's will.

Attempts have been made to identify features of Hancock's work from known examples; these include exotic birds, fruits, Chinese subjects, trees with extended branches on one side over one or two persons sitting or reclining, scenes with water and ruins, swans and reeds in the foreground, and sporting subjects. It must be remembered, however, that these were popular subjects of the day and much copying and adapting was practised. Among other original works, Hancock adapted paintings by such artists as Watteau, Bouchet and Lancret.

When we consider the great output of inferior quality enamels at Bilston, it is evident that some less-skilled engravers found employment here, and, naturally, they were less expensive to engage. The transfer prints on some of the small oval patch boxes and ' presentation ' boxes, having a simple picture with wording above or below, are rather crude, but, of course, they were meant to be sold at a cheap price. If these engravers and their assistants lacked originality in design, they could make use of books of illustrations and patterns available. One such was ' The Ladies Amusement or the Whole Art of Japanning made easy '.[10] This had nearly one thousand five hundred designs on some two hundred plates, and Robert Hancock was responsible for some of them. With no copyright laws in force other people's work could be copied or modified at will.

REFERENCES
[1] W. Chaffers, ' Marks and Monograms on Pottery and Porcelain ', 3rd Edition, p. 978.
[2] Eric Benton, T.E.C.C., 1970.
[3] H. W. Hughes, ' Authorship of Some Designs on Porcelain and Enamel and Robert Hancock's Connection with Battersea and Bow '. T.E.C.C., 1935.
[4] ' Louis F. Boitard and his designs on Battersea Enamels ', T.E.C.C., 1932. A. J. Toppin, ' Notes on Jannsen and the Artists of the Battersea Factory ', T.E.C.C., 1932. C. Cook, ' Simon Francois Ravenet and his Engravings on Battersea Enamels ', T.E.C.C., 1955.
[5] C. Cook, ' The Art of Hancock ', T.E.C.C., 1947.
[6] Ibid.
[7] F. W. Hackwood, ' Oldbury and Round About ', pp. 303-306.
[8] T.E.C.C., 1947. Also, ' Supplement to the Life and Work of Robert Hancock ', T.E.C.C., 1955.
[9] A. J. Toppin, ' Robert Hancock and His Sons ', T.E.C.C., 1934.
[10] W. Chaffers, ' Marks and Monograms on Pottery and Porcelain ', 3rd Edition, p. 978.

10

THE RANGE OF THE
ENAMELLERS' WORK

REFERENCE has been made to the toymakers and boxmakers of the first half of the 18th century, their products were essential to the enamellers who, of course, were often manufacturers also. There were small workshops which concentrated on the manufacture of boxes, trinkets, and such items, and their owners taught the skills and techniques to their apprentices or their own children. Among men so engaged and not mentioned previously we find[1]:—

Matthew Birch	1750	Thomas Wooley	1750
William Taylor	1756	Richard Pendrill	1756
John Lawley	1757	William Barker	1757
Joseph Robinson	1757	William Spooner	1758
Benjamin Mason	1758	Joseph Langson	1758
George Archer	1759	John Corbett	1761
William Hare	1762	Thomas Lowe	1763
Richard Acton	1764	John Davies	1769
Thomas Cordwell	1769	John Dean	1771
Benjamin Barber	1771		

All the above took apprentices of both sexes, and there were probably others working alone. In addition it must be remembered that the buckle-makers and chape-forgers continued in business throughout the century and the work of hinge-makers, mount-turners and the like was in great demand both in and beyond Bilston; Hackwood[2] states, for instance, that the Wednesbury enamellers had to obtain nearly all their metal fittings such as box-hinges and salt cellar rims from Bilston and, no doubt, some custom came from Birmingham. The work of all these craftsmen was expertly done: box-lids fitted perfectly without needing a catch, hinges were neat and most carefully attached, sections or parts, of candle sticks, for example, were inconspicuously joined.[3]

There was a great variety of work produced by the enamellers to meet the desires and tastes of the age and a willingness to make, in cheaper form, copies of continental innovations perhaps made in gold or other precious metal.[4] The commonest objects produced were small boxes of one sort or another and of these the snuff-box was a favourite.

The taking of snuff was a popular habit. We are familiar with the ritual involved and practised by the dandies of the day as they took the air in the streets of such towns as London or Bath, or met their friends in the coffee house, gaming club or salon. To us it appears incredible that there were 'schools' to teach the art of offering and taking snuff, with almost as many do's and don'ts as in the fashionable studios of the dancing masters.

At the other end of the scale, we have the rough workman, in his local ale-house, using a snuff box, for they were made for sale at all sorts of prices, from guineas to pence, from a beautiful enamelled gold box with a lovely painted lid (suitable for a royal gift, a similar type in silver, or the common copper-based variety which could vary from one with a well-executed painted lid and sides to a plain transfer printed box.[5] The lids frequently had pictures based on incidents from classical mythology, with representations of gods and goddesses in stories familiar to their owners. Classical ruins, rustic scenes and characters, sea and landscapes and sporting itmes were typical subjects for the box painters.

Since the ladies also enjoyed taking their pinches of snuff, some dainty boxes were made to appeal to their taste. Queen Charlotte herself indulged in the habit, having her own favourite brands, and so set the fashion for ladies of the court and others to follow if they were so inclined.

The gold and silver boxes were mostly made in London and Birmingham by goldsmiths and silversmiths. In July 1750, Thomas Gill of Moor Street, Birmingham was advertising that he 'makes and sells tools for gold and silversmiths . . . and snuff box makers'. They could employ an artist in enamelling or painter of miniatures on ivory to supply lids or insets for lids; a number of highly skilled miniaturists were at work at the time such as Richard Cosway, Jeremiah Meyer, John Smart and others.

Another type of box highly popular at the time was the patch-box; these small boxes, usually oval or round, were much in favour. They contained 'dots' of colour which the lady applied to her face in spots of her own choosing. The 'patch' consisted of a tiny circle of black velvet or silk with an adhesive on the back and to put it in exactly the right place she needed a mirror. So we find one fixed inside the lid. The early patch boxes had a mirror of polished steel, but later on, around about 1785, the boxmakers learned how to attach a piece of glass instead. The beaux also, at one period, indulged in the fashion and some of the ladies, as is often the case with fashion, went to extremes, evoking satirical comments. Oliver Goldsmith wrote that they put patches on every part of the face except the tip of the nose. It is quite probable that, when the fashion for patches on the face went out of favour, some of the small boxes with mirrors inside were used by the ladies for other purposes, as snuff boxes or containers of odds and ends, as a mirror, however small, was always useful to have at hand. Here again there is great diversity in the shapes and sizes. Many of those produced in Bilston had a rather crude transfer print, unpainted, on the lid and one colour only, such as pink or green, on the sides. Some of the smaller boxes without mirrors were frequently used for other purposes, for holding pills, for instance. Examples of these boxes in the Bilston collection include the following:—
A small circular box with 'Thou hast worth and merit' printed on the lid.
A blue one with 'Love for Love'.
An oval box $1\frac{3}{4}$ inches long with 'Sacred to Friendship'. This has a pink body.
There are also items of better quality with painted pictures on the lids and floral sprays and designs on fluted sides over the base of white enamel.

Another popular box of the day was the bonbonnière, as its name suggests an import from France. This was less a box for holding 'bonbons' than for perfumed cachous. When one remembers that bad state into which the teeth of even the well-to-do deteriorated and the low standard of oral hygiene, the need for a 'breath sweetener' is evident. These boxes were made in a variety of shapes, the makers indulging their fancy in all sorts of interesting forms following the shapes, for example, of the egg, orange, or lemon. Other boxes, popular in the period 1770-1785 approximately were those stamped from such a mould as of a sleeping swan, cat or dog head, fruit or bird. They are usually brightly coloured and carefully painted and fetch high prices today. One box for example, is in the form of a sleeping swan with black and red markings, lying on a blue base painted with reeds, the lid painted with swans on a lake. This is about three inches long and in 1963 was valued at over £200.[6] When the top of the box had such an irregular shape the hinged lid had to be at the base and again the skill of the workmen is evident in the natural forms and colouring they achieved.

A number of enamelled objects might be found on the dressing table in a lady's boudoir: a scent bottle, bodkin case, scissors case, candlesticks for illumination and an étui. Here again we note the French influence, an étui being a small lidded case for holding such items as tweezers, nail file, penknife, tooth-pick, compasses and a six inch rule. It is somewhat puzzling to find this last item, but it may have been used in arranging elaborate hair styles.

The outsides of the étuis were finely enamelled, having deli-cately painted scenes set in pretty surrounds, sometimes with raised gilt scroll borders and matching lids; gilt metal mounts are common and the use of gold on white was popular. The various contents of the étui fitted neatly into their respective compartments inside.

Scent bottles were treated similarly; one in the Bilston collection has flattened sides painted in yellow, purple and pink panels. There is a raised white diaper pattern with small floral designs set in a raised gilt surround. The stopper has a finial in the form of a bird. This scent bottle was purchased from Sotheby's, from the Gerald Mander collection, in 1961, for £72. Herbert Read in a paper read to the English Ceramic Circle in 1932 dealing with ' Cross Currents in English Porcelain, Glass and Enamels' suggests that some of the glass scent bottles, previously attributed to Bristol or London, may have been made in Stour-bridge or Birmingham glass factories and painted in South Staffordshire. This would provide additional work for the box painters.

With candles as the principal means of lighting, pairs of candlesticks were in great demand,[7] and painted in white enamel and then decorated with coloured designs both on the base section and the stem they were very pleasing in appearance. Owing to the limited size of the muffle they were done in sections and then the pieces joined most inconspicuously.

Enamelled watch and clock faces are frequently found and also transfer-printed small square or oblong calendars on box lids. The amount of detail, in the latter, in such a small space, speaks highly of the skill of both the engraver and the man who did the transfer on to the lid. The lady of the house might possess an enamelled brooch, while her husband might have about the house an enamelled pen-and-ink stand, a playing-card tray with pictures of the suits, and, on the sideboard, decanter labels with 'Claret', 'Burgundy', 'Rum' and so forth, spelled out in black Gothic lettering. He might also possess an enamelled tobacco box, and canes with enamelled heads were sometimes carried.

The walls of the hall, withdrawing and other rooms might carry enamelled plaques which frequently consisted of head and shoulder pictures of family or national figures, such war heroes as admirals or generals, actresses and other notable ladies of the day. The same subjects are found on medallions and small plaques of two or three inches in length. George III, Queen Charlotte, members of the Royal Family, Admirals Nelson and Rodney, Generals Cornwallis and George Washington were subjects, among others, which found favour.

Other subjects of a more domestic nature were available in painted enamel: caskets, tea caddies, sugar canisters, salt cellars, egg-cups, door knobs, finger plates, nutmeg-graters, hand candlesticks and thimbles. Various little boxes, such as the souvenir type, could be put to several uses as containers for small items.

In the finest examples of these products we realise how much they belong to their period, when elegance, fine taste and artistic feeling were expressed in buildings, furniture, and objets d'art, and when the beauty of the completed work counted more than the time spent on making it.

REFERENCES

1 Apprentice Lists, Wolv. R.L.
2 'Wednesbury Workshops', p. 128.
3 G. B. Hughes, 'English Snuff Boxes', pp. 73-74.
4 B. Rackham, 'Porcelain as a sidelight on Battersea Enamels', T.E.C.C., 1932.
5 G. B. Hughes, 'English Snuff Boxes', Ch. 6.
6 When the Bilston collection was valued by Sotheby's.
7 G. B. Hughes, 'Battersea and South Staffordshire Enamels', in 'Collecting Antiques', p. 29.

11

THE ALLIED TRADES

IT is difficult to say that a particular box maker did, or did not,
extend his work to include some enamelling, especially if he
were only engaged in business in a small way. Nevertheless the
output of these men was essential and something of their histories
should be given.

ALLEN

THERE were two families of this name in Bilston by the year
1700, but the one we are concerned with is that of Thomas
Allen. The names of Thomas Allen, Elizabeth his wife and a
son Joseph are on the Parish Register for the year 1695. In the
same year a son, Thomas, was born. He was an ordinary working-class man, first a chape forger and later a bucklemaker, for,
in that capacity, he took an apprentice, John Shale of Bilston,
in 1701. Later he turned to the making of 'toys' and did so
successfully, for in 1713 he took John Ballard, from Abbots
Morton as an apprentice and Martin Ballard, obviously a relative, from Northwich in 1715. Perhaps they were cousins and
the outcome of John's apprenticeship influenced the parents of
Martin to send him to the same master.

Thomas Allen served as Constable in 1742. His son Joseph,
born in 1695, had, one concludes, worked in his father's shop for
he took Francis Bailey as an apprentice to learn the trade of
toy maker in 1721. More interesting, however, is the fact, that
in 1718 Joseph Allen is described as a japanner—one of the two
earliest in Bilston. He is also thus described when his daughter,
Elizabeth, was christened on March 13th 1719, but in later entries
of his children Ames describes him as a toymaker; for Joseph
1720, Josiah 1722 and William 1724, and in 1726 there is an
additional 'side-line' of distiller.

The fact that he was a toymaker and japanner would lead us to assume that he possibly took the next step and added enamelling to his activities and so found employment for a painter in the two allied crafts. There is an entry in the Court Roll for 1761 referring to 'Thomas Allen of Wolverhampton, son of Joseph Allen deceased, who was the eldest son of Thomas Allen here-to-fore of the liberty of Bilston, Chape forger '.

Ames mentions a Matthew Allen, who had sons Joseph 1736, John 1737, and Benjamin 1740 and 1742, as a bucklemaker; others with workshops included James, a chaper, who took A. Bratt as an apprentice in 1744, and Thomas, a chape filer who took Mary and Sarah Perry as apprentices in 1760. The latter is probably the same Thomas referred to above. In addition a Thomas Allen, toymaker, accepted Elizabeth Woolley as an apprentice in 1764. This man was probably the son who was born to Matthew in 1734. It is reasonable to conclude that there was some family connection and co-operation in business interests.

COOPER

THERE were two families of the name Cooper in Bilston by 1700, the fathers being Richard and Joseph. Richard was a locksmith and when he died in 1710 he left to his eldest son, William, ' all those my Shoppe, Tools and Household goods which are now in his possession ' while the younger son John, received forty pounds. It is recorded that he had two apprentices in 1695, namely Richard Leese and Richard Hale. It is Cooper's son, John, born in 1689 who interests us for he was a bucklemaker and later a toymaker, in which capacity he accepted James Fletcher in 1732. In a list of pew allocations it seems that he was also the inn keeper of the White Horse. He was Constable in 1734 and took an active part in affairs of the church and town. An interesting item indicative of life in those days was that in 1732 John Cooper received a small payment for sparrow heads and there are similar entries referring to other people from time to time. The William who died in 1732, called a toymaker in his will, was probably his brother, but there is no reference to him leaving a workshop or tools. As a bucklemaker, William took William Marston of Wednesbury as an apprentice. He was baptized by Ames in 1722 at the age of eighteen as he had been the son of Anabaptists.

John Cooper died in 1747 and his will is of interest. To his son Richard he left forty pounds, and ten pounds to each of his three daughters. To his eldest son, John, he bequeathed ' all shop tools of all kinds, only one voyce excepted for my son Richard Cooper '. He declares that his son John ' stands indebted to me by bond of one hundred and twenty pounds '. John is probably the man referred to in the 1771 Land List as in possession of four small pieces which included Cooper's Croft and Cooper's Lunts. Richard, who received one vice in his father's will is probably the locksmith who died in 1762. If so he does not appear to have been very successful for he left one shilling to his son William; the younger children were not mentioned. On the other hand this Richard Cooper may have been the son of the locksmith who died in 1710. In 1731 Richard Cooper married Anne Green whose brother was Edward Green, bucklemaker, and so became related to John the boxmaker and enameller, her other brother.

In the 1781 Directory, John Cooper is listed as a brass-founder and ironmonger and a Joseph Cooper as a chapemaker. It is reasonable to conclude that the Coopers built up thriving business and their descendants are listed in the Commercial Directory for 1818-19-20 and Smart's Directory of Wolverhampton for 1827 as follows:—

T. T. Cooper of Bridge Street, Brass founder.
James Cooper of Bridge Street, Factor and Brass founder.
George Cooper of Stafford Street, Ironmaster.
Thomas Cooper of Oxford Street, Japanner.

Timothy Turner Cooper paid thirteen pounds levy for his house and shop, which suggests that the family business may have been in existence in Bridge Street for a long time together with the businesses of several members of the Beckett family. Thomas Cooper the japanner probably had his business in Oxford Street but he owned houses in Hall Street, Lichfield Street and Mount Pleasant. Oxford Street was a newly developed straight road, cutting out Bridge Street, so the japanning shop was probably built to the latest requirements of the trade. He was still there in 1833. It is interesting to note that a family japanning work was in existence in Oxford Street until very recently and in the last two or three years the old buildings have

been demolished to make way for a new Oxford Street.
In the Commercial Directory, a George Cooper is listed as an ironmonger in Church Street. From the Levy List it would appear that this is where he lived, assuming he is the same man who had a works in Stafford Street. He was also still in business in 1833 as was James, the brass founder, in Bridge Street. Other Coopers in Bilston in the first half of the eighteenth century included Benjamin, who was a locksmith, George, a chape forger, Joseph, a bucklemaker and Cornelius, chape forger and bucklemaker. Cornelius was not very successful as a chape forger. When he died in 1728, Ames called him ' poor ', an unusual entry.

It is almost impossible to sort out the various Coopers as the same Christian names recur again and again. For example, we find many Richards and there was a Thomas who had two sons Isaac (1740) and Benjamin (1743) who were jointly penalised with a forty pound bond in a paternity case in 1763. The William Cooper who was Chapel Warden in 1741 and who bought two seats in the Chapel (1733) ' late now in the Tenure of Benjamin Bickley ' would appear to be Richard's eldest son and John's brother and concerned with the family business. He owned a small property of about an acre near John Wilkinson's estate, which he let.

PINSON

THE first Pinson of interest is the John Pinson who married Sarah Taylor in 1707 and Elizabeth Latchford in 1716. He was another versatile craftsman who is described both as a bucklemaker (1719) and toymaker (1728). He was Constable in 1729 and when he died his personal estate amounted to £143.13s.6d. Letters of administration were granted to his widow in 1740. There are references to a casting shop, four pairs of flasks and boards, sand tubs and ' the stamp frame at £1.10s.0d '.

His son John, born in 1720, carried on with and extended the business, for it was as a boxmaker that he took Thomas Sakelin as an apprentice in 1748. His chief output was snuff boxes of various shapes and sizes and we are fortunate that details of his shop and equipment are given in the inventory made at the time of his death in 1751. These included:—

' Goods in casting shop, utensils for casting ... £3. 8s.6d.
Goods in workshops—8 vices, 2 hand vices ... £2. 7s.6d.

1 anvil	...	£1.12s.6d.
1 draw bench and tools thereto belonging	...	3s.6d.
1 pair shop bellows	...	£1. 1s.0d.
3 laythes	...	£2.17s.6d.
1 pair shears and other shop tools	... ...	5s.0d.
4 Vice benches	... ...	3s.6d.
In Stamp house, stamps and dies ...	... ...	£2.10s.0d. '

Item two, with the plural 'workshops', suggests at least a number of employees. Another item is 'Mettle Snuff Boxes, old lumber and things unseen 3s.6d.', and again 'mettle boxes, finished and unfinished £71.10s.0d.' When one considers the value placed on the equipment, this shows a considerable output. With Pinson, we have another instance of a 'sideline', for a number of items to do with brewing are listed including 259 gallons of beer at 9d. per gallon! The total of the inventory was £154.9s.4d. John Pinson had some connections with the nearby Parish of Penn—his wife probably came from there—for the Burial Register has the following entries:—

17.10.1740   Elizabeth d. of John Pinson of Bilston.
30. 6.1747   William s. of John Pinson of Bilston.
20. 3.1751   John s. of John and Elizabeth Pinson.
31. 5.1751   John Pinson of Billstone.

The above William was the son baptized at Bilston in 1744, and Elizabeth's birth was also recorded by the Revd. Best in the Bilston Register, 23.8.1746.

By marriage the Pinsons were associated with some of the earliest experimenters in japanning and enamelling; a Mary Pinson married Samuel Stone in 1718. He was a japanner and ironmonger of whom more will be written. Another of the same name married George Perry in 1735; he was a toymaker and father of an enameller.

A third John Pinson (born 1753) to a John and Abigail could only be, at best, a relative of the above men but may have worked in their shops. On the other hand, a John Pinson served as a Surveyor of the Highways in 1745, but he is called a hopseller. He could have been the father of another John born to John and Isabel Pinson in 1741. He is possibly the John Pinson buried in January 1772, and the absence of entries in the registers of both births and burials suggests that the family of boxmakers left Bilston some time after 1751; no Pinson was owning or letting any land in 1771.

STONE

EARLY in the eighteenth century there was, in Bilston, a
Thomas Stone described by Ames as a toymaker, but more
important was Samuel Stone the elder who was a japanner, one
of the earliest. He died in 1724 leaving a son Samuel and some
younger children, one of whom, Thomas, was born in 1702. His
estate realised only £13.4s.0d. and his eldest son received only
one shilling but probably control of the shop. Samuel was twenty-
nine when his father died and he developed the business, having
much of the drive and energy of men like Benjamin Bickley. As
already mentioned, he married Mary Pinson in 1718. He was
working as a japanner before his father's death and later extended
his interests. He seems to have acted as a supplier of metals for
the various trades in the town; for example he bought rolled
plate of a new alloy—4 tons in 1743 and 8 tons in 1750.

He was prominent in the affairs of the town and church,
serving as Constable in 1731 and he was very keen on the
improvement and development of turn-pike roads which were so
necessary owing to the rapid increase in trade, particularly the
movement of coal to such places as Birmingham. An example
of his concern is seen in that he advanced the necessary money
in 1737 for ' the repair of the street in Bilston '. The balance of
£8.8s.0d. was paid to him in 1746. The fact that he does not
appear to have had any apprentices may indicate that the japanning side of his business interests became subordinate to that of
agent and stockholder.

He was sufficiently successful to turn to the purchase of
property and in 1733, writes Lawley, the Old Cross House—which
was used to signify that a town had the right to hold a market
—was altered to hold prisoners in the lower part; in 1738 the
building was leased to Stone for thirty pounds and, apparently,
it ceased to be used for parish purposes. Ames mentioned an
old document which showed that there were two Crosses in
Bilston, ' The Nether-cross where Jon Roberts and his wife now
live, and the Over-cross (hard by Willm. Smith's)'. In 1739 Stone
was in dispute with the wealthy and old-established Robyns
family over a piece of land which fronted Bilston Street and Pin-
fold Street and the mansion house of the Robyns. As plaintiff
he submitted a plan at the Stafford Assizes in 1739.[1]

104

Samuel Stone's wife died in 1748 and in the burial entry he is called 'gent.' He may have retired a few years later or gone into other business. He died in May 1760 and the entry in the register reads ' Samuel Stone, gent. He acquired a very plentiful fortune by trade from a small beginning and died in the sixty sixth year of his age '.

One of his brothers, not named in the father's will, was probably the Stephen Stone who married Ann Moss in 1740. She came from a family associated with buckles and toys; a Mary Moss had been apprenticed to Thomas Shale, a bucklemaker and toymaker, in 1730. Stephen was about seventeen years younger than Samuel and another brother, Thomas, also his senior, became a toymaker. Stephen, as a toymaker himself, took Henry Griffin as an apprentice in 1744. He had a son John (1753) and Stephen (1755), and he is probably the man listed in the Levy Book of 1770 as owning some fifty four acres of land, some with coal seams beneath. He died in 1786.

That there were other families of the same name in Bilston is clear from the descendants of Thomas, the early toymaker, and from the fact that the will of John Cooper, toymaker, in 1747 was witnessed by both Samuel and John Stone. Moreover a second Samuel Stone died in the same year as ' the gent.' Three Stones are recorded in the 1771 Land Survey, including Stephen who owned the Quarry Croft and John who rented out four pieces of land; in addition we find that a William Stone died in 1767 and a Thomas in 1773. Stephen Stone owned a quarry near the Coseley boundary and is called a quarryman in the 1781 Directory. Taking into account the number of men and their business and family connections, might it not be assumed that there were some exeperiments with enamelling? At least part of the family remained in Bilston for a John Stone was a Surveyor of the Highways in the 1795 list and again in 1811.

EATON

THE Eatons are another example of development and diversity of occupation during the eighteenth century with corresponding increase, or sometimes decrease, in the family fortunes. Ames included a William Eaton and his wife Ann in the 1695 Register, but no children are named. Ann Eaton is described as a Papist in 1705.

Children could have been born subsequently to William, but there was also a Richard Eaton called a collier when he married Elizabeth Sharp in 1692. This Richard Eaton would appear to be the man described by Ames in the burial register for the 13th of January 1728 as a ' groover ' or collier, and he was buried at Bilston. He is probably the same Richard Eaton who was listed among people who had ' slipped into ' the town when the Chapel Wardens conducted a search in 1689, and ' surreptiously gain'd a Settlement here '. It was the offspring of these who were the Richard Eaton, born in 1697, who became a bucklemaker and collier, and Joseph, born in 1700 who became a bucklemaker also. Richard married Hannah Taylor in 1723, and it is interesting to note that at least two Taylors were working as toymakers in Bilston and took apprentices; a second Hannah Taylor learned the trade of boxpainter under Thomas Bayliss from 1755 onwards.

Joseph developed the toymaking side of the business; in pariular the increasing demand for boxes of all shapes and sizes attracted him and he could supply the requirements of his friends. In 1743 he could afford to pay thirteen pounds for a pew in the chapel, along with such men as Benjamin Bickley and Isaac Beckett. He was Chapel Warden in 1739, 1746 and 1748 and served as a Surveyor of the Highways in 1743 and 1760. Another office he held was that of Constable in 1750, while in 1751 and again in 1766 he was one of the two Land Tax collectors in the town. Joseph had a long life; his wife Margaret died in 1781 and he survived for another two years. He had two sons, Thomas, born in 1728 and Joseph in 1741. Ames calls him a bucklemaker in the 1728 entry, at which date he would be about twenty eight years old, and the extension of his business came later.

It is probable that Richard Eaton was working with Joseph for he is called a toymaker in 1759. He also took public office being an Overseer of the Poor in 1739 and 1741. Another Eaton —Thomas—was Constable in 1765, and he was one of the two executors of John Bickley's will in 1776. He was probably Joseph's son born in 1728 but it would seem that he was not directly concerned with toymaking or enamelling as he was appointed Surgeon and Apothecary to the Workhouse in 1762. Twenty years later he was no longer resident in Bilston but living at Agardsley Park, Hanbury, Staffs. for he testified that he had received, in her own writing, the will of Mary Ames from Mrs. Catharine Bickley, at whose home she died. Here again we find the close co-operation between the families of toymakers and enamellers. Other pointers to this are available. For example, why should an entry in the burial register read ' 19th Sept. 1760 Eaton Green, the son of Thomas and Betty '? This is a most unusual name to give to a boy, but then it is recalled that there was a prominent enameller named John Green in Bilston at the time, and some link between the two families is obvious. In fact a Thomas Green married Betty Eaton in 1757.

We have no knowledge of the occupations of the other Eaton men, but a John Eaton died in 1762 and a Peter Eaton in 1790. A George Eaton had a daughter Hannah baptized in 1749. One who was not very successful was the Richard Eaton who died in 1772. He was chape maker by trade. In his will he left one shilling each to his brothers William, Joseph and John; the personal estate being under five pounds. Some Eatons appear to have prospered for the 1833 Directory by Bridgen of Wolverhampton gives ' Mr. Eaton, Market Street '. White's Directory for 1834 has an interesting entry under Bilston as follows: ' Captain James Eaton, R.N. Stafford Street '. He would appear to be the same gentleman who had lived in Market Street.

MOSS

WRITING in 1695, Ames gives the spelling of this family name as Mosse and as such identifies a Robert Mosse with sons John, Jeremy and Robert and also, in the home of Roger and Esther Dovey apparently, Joseph, John and James Mosse who might well have been orphaned relatives. There was also at this time, a John Moss who was a ' whitesmith '; in 1705 he took Thomas Duce for a five year apprenticeship and Duce's sister, Elizabeth, married James Moss in 1709. It is probable that the Overseers had to place some young members of the Moss family, for in addition to John who went to George Fenney, a Joseph joined Robert Wildsmith, bagweaver, in 1725 till he was twenty four years old, and a James was taken by Edward Mason, tiemaker, in 1728 till the same age. Robert Moss was a bucklemaker, chafemaker and gunlocksmith. He died in 1729. John was also a gunlocksmith while James became a bucklemaker. In 1721 John Moss had been apprenticed to George Fenney, a bucklemaker of Wolverhampton until he was twenty one years of age. He was probably the son born to John in 1714. A Mary Moss was apprenticed to another Bilston bucklemaker, Thomas Shale, in 1730 until she was twenty four. Both of these children were indentured by the Parish.

A Moss with more agricultural interests was the Joseph Moss who married a Bilston girl, Elizabeth Stotten, in 1707. He was a flax dresser but that does not exclude him from other work typical of that of his contemporaries. The inventory of his possessions in 1731 realised over three hundred pounds. In his will, his eldest son was named as Joseph. The will was witnessed by Esther Dovey who made her mark; she had three boys of the name Moss living with her when Ames made his list of parishioners in 1695 and who became connected with the leading enamellers and others through marriages. This Joseph was probably the man who shared pew No. 39 with Sir Richard Wrottesley, and whose widow later paid £6.10s.0d. for seat No. 45 in 1733.

The man we are most concerned with here is the William Moss who was a bucklemaker principally, but who did other work in association with the enamellers. He was most probably the son born to Joseph and Elizabeth in 1714, for he had an elder brother, also Joseph, born in 1712. William's wife, Mary, bore him several sons; William in 1741, Thomas in 1751 and Benjamin in 1752. He left the latter two sons £220 between them when he died in 1775. He also mentions Joseph, another son, to whom he left a shilling only since he had done quite well earlier on and better than the other two. He was Constable in 1766 and his close friendship with the two principal enamellers of the day is seen in the fact that he witnessed Benjamin Bickley's will and also, as a widower, married Elizabeth Beckett in 1769. His wife Mary died in 1760. Bickley's widow, Mary, left £20 to William Moss, bucklemaker, but her will was not proved until 1780.

It would seem that, at a time when infant mortality was so great, the three Moss children living with Esther Dovey all survived, for a Joseph married in 1734, James in 1742, and John in 1749. A reference is made in the Wolverhampton Register of Marriages to another William Moss: July 10th 1765, Edward

Moss, minor, s. of William Moss and Hanah Foxhall. This could be the William Moss, draper, who in 1783 entered into a bond with Isaac Beckett and not the William above. He was in Bilston at the same time, as the baptism register shows, for he had two sons, Joseph and Edward, by his wife Elizabeth in 1743 and 1746. This would make Edward about nineteen when he married as a minor.

ILLEDGE

SOME members of this family, also spelt Illidge, lived in Wolverhampton, but in the 1720s two lived in Bilston. They were both weavers named William and Francis. Another one, John Illedge, was described as a bucklemaker in 1724 when a daughter was baptised. In the previous year he had married Elizabeth Mousell who was related to Benjamin Bickley's mother, Susannah Mousell. Elizabeth could have been Susannah's daughter or Clement Mousell's. Both of these, Susannah who was a widow, and Clement, had a son named John and it was one of these boys who was apprenticed to a whitesmith in 1701.

Returning to John Illedge, we find he had a son John born in 1730. Apparently the business thrived and in 1748 he was a Surveyor of the Highways. He died in 1752. The younger John then expanded the business and extended it. Having worked with his father as a bucklemaker, he took John Milward, in 1752, to serve an apprenticeship to the age of twenty one. As a toymaker he accepted Joseph Marcrom in 1758 and John Hemming in 1760, the latter until he reached the age of twenty four. These three boys were placed by the parish. Of his own sons, four died young, but John, born in 1756 survived. It is probable that Illedge did not remain in Bilston but joined relatives in Wolverhampton who continued in business. In 1781 William is called a brassfounder, and in 1818 Thomas Illedge is described as a japanner of St. James' Square.

LINTON

THIS family had a long connection with Bilston for about three hundred years from the time of Henry VIII.[2] At the beginning of the eighteenth century there were Joseph, Benjamin and Thomas; the latter died at Wolverhampton in 1702 leaving a son Joseph. Joseph is not included in the Bilston Register for 1695 but there is a page missing; he was, however, on the 1699 list of Customary Tenants: 'Joseph Linton holdeth a customary tenement where he now dwells, also a customary tenement called Stone Pit House'. The latter would seem to be the family home, and Lawley states that it stood in what is now called Oatmeal Square and was called Stone Croft House. It was nearly opposite the old Manor House in High Street, now the Greyhound Inn. Stone was quarried in the land south of the house which the Lintons owned; this was known as Stonefield Quarry. The name Stonefield has continued to the present day; three schools built in this area were given that name.

Joseph Linton was the prominent member of the family. He acted as Chapel Warden in 1705 and a Serving Bailiff in 1716. On three occasions, between 1717 and 1724, he is described as a yeoman though it is probable that he had a workshop. It was his son, Joseph, born in 1713 who, Freeman claims,[3] was one of the last bucklemakers in Bilston. Another son, John, became a boxmaker, so described when he died in 1747. It was Benjamin's son, John, who could be the more humble chapemaker who died in 1730. In his will he mentions John Whitehouse, a hingemaker, and this man would have supplied hinges, no doubt, to John and other Lintons who appear to have arrived in Bilston in the 1730s. When enamelling was flourishing there were Joseph, William, two Benjamins, Orlando, Thomas and Simeon and among these there could well have been a toymaker or enameller.

It is a strange thing that there is a complete absence of marriages of Linton men in the Wolverhampton Register in the first thirty years of the century; then we find that of Joseph and Ann Duce in 1734. She was a Bilston girl and the niece of William Duce who died 'a prisoner in ye Fleet att London in 1705'. How he came to be there we do not know.

Another interesting marriage was that of Simeon, Joseph's son born in 1738, who appears to have married his cousin, Elizabeth Linton in 1774.

It was the descendants of Joseph the 'yeoman' who probably were most successful in business and, according to Freeman, the family moved to Tettenhall, a pleasant village beyond Wolverhampton, when the Industrial Revolution was changing the appearance of Bilston.

STOKES

IT has already been noted that the frequent use of a few common Christian names causes difficulty in sorting out the various family connections and relationships; the Stoke family is no exception. At the beginning of the eighteenth century we find Joseph Stokes called a 'new comer' in the 1699 Lord of the Manor's Chief Rent Book. He was a Roman Catholic or Anabaptist, for his son John, born in 1697, was included in the list of children not baptized according to the rites of the Church of England. He moved to Dudley, a few miles away, in 1701.

The 1695 Register shows Thomas Stokes occupying the same house as Roger, his wife Sarah and children Thomas and Daniel, who lost his sight in 1703. With them was Will Stokes, while another, Thomas, was servant to Mr. John Hoo and 'living in'. Thomas, the house-holder, is described as a locksmith in 1703; his children were not baptized by the curate and a fine was paid, two shillings in the case of Sarah in 1698. The Stoke family had workshops typical of the kind developing in Bilston in the 1720s. There were two named Thomas then, as can be seen from the following entries in 1727:—

May 12th   Stokes Thomas s. of Thos., Gunlockmaker.
Oct. 8th   Stokes Thomas s. of Tho., Steel Mill maker.

This is also evident in the list of the 'Inhabitants of Bilston Chapelry' in 1718, which distinguishes between Thomas Stokes and Tho. Stokes.

Ames records, under the same name, in addition, a bucklemaker, toymaker and blacksmith and it seems reasonable to conclude that the two men could, at different times, have been working at these trades, bucklemaker to toymaker being a probable development. Other Stokes occupations were John Stokes wood screw maker, Joseph a toymaker, and William a bucklemaker. All these were at work in the 1720-30 period.

One Thomas Stokes died in 1731; he appears to be the man who married Elizabeth Perry, also of Bilston, in 1696. It was his children, presumably, who were not baptized by Ames, for we know that some of the Perrys were Catholics. He seems to have prospered and in his will he is called 'yeoman'. His personal

111

estate amounted to £228.2s.6d. and he left money to his wife Elizabeth, sons Daniel, Isaac and Joseph and he left £60 to his daughter Elizabeth. Isaac, in addition, was to receive 'all my shop tools'; this suggests that he had been managing the workshop in the later years.

Thomas the locksmith died in 1741 and he was the more prominent one who added extra workshop enterprises to his original trade. He could, indeed, be the bucklemaker and toymaker. He was concerned with land exchanges with William Robins, a big landowner, in the Bilston 'open fields' in 1719 and 1722.[1] He was Constable in 1739 and the Lord of the Manor's Bailiff in 1740. Apparently he had neither wife nor children for he left to his brother John 'all the tyths and tenths whatsoever of his Copyhold land in the parish of Sedgley'.

He mentions his brother Daniel with whom he had made arrangements regarding his mother and the disposal of property. The residue of his estate was bequeathed to his uncle Daniel Stokes and his two brothers-in-law to dispose of among his relatives; one of the two was William Cooper, the bucklemaker and toymaker. It must be the descendants of the Thomas Stokes who died in 1731 who carried on the work into the second half of the century. An interesting one is the John Stokes who became apprentice to William Cox, the Wolverhampton box painter; he could have been the son born to Francis and Sarah Stokes in 1749. He would, during his years of apprenticeship, become familiar with the technique of enamelling.

In the period when this trade was flourishing in Bilston the following had workshops there, but of none can it be said with certainty that he was an enameller: Francis, the bucklemaker and toymaker's son, Charles, probably his brother, and inevitably, the two Thomases born in 1727. A new comer was Nathaniel, while Isaac, son of the yeoman, carried on in the workshop of his late father, his brother Daniel having died in 1744.

None of them appears to have been very successful; no children, except the boy who went to Cox, are recorded as serving apprenticeships and none of them seems to have taken apprentices himself. Their names are not found in the directories and the only sign of any ownership of property is in the 1771 Land Survey which has a 'Widow Stokes' owning some seven acres called 'Stoke's Three Wet Furlongs'. There may be a connection here with the Thomas who married Jane Taylor.

DAVIES

THE difficulties arising from the repeition of the same Christian name are reversed here because we have 'Davies' and 'Davis' used, and apparently sometimes indiscriminately. With entries being written in registers at both Wolverhampton and Bilston, and uneducated parents giving their names, obviously the spelling is not always reliable. However, in the first decade of the eighteenth century, Robert Davies was working as a bucklemaker and two men named John Davis had workshops. Between 1716 and 1730 we find the following recorded. All of these had the surname 'Davies':—

Joseph	toymaker	1723 and 1728
Isaac	toymaker	1725
	boxmaker	1728
Charles	toymaker	1726
Thomas	toymaker	1727 and 1729
Edward	boxmaker	1718, 1720 and 1726
Richard	boxmaker	1720
John	gunlock maker	1719 and 1721
Robert (jnr.)	bucklemaker	1721

John Davies took Amos Davis as an apprentice in 1730 and he also was a boxmaker. The boxmaker Edward Davis, who died in 1751, would appear to be the man who married Ann Dovey in 1713, for in his will he refers to some property in Kidderminster bequeathed to him in the will of John Dovey, a mason in that town. We see here a probable connection with Dovey Hawksford.

Earlier than this, John Davies the boxmaker had been one of the first to be buried in the newly consecrated churchyard (1727) which Ames had worked so assiduously to secure for the town, and two months later Thomas Davies, 'a Journeyman Bucklemaker' was also interred there. Robert the bucklemaker had already died, and Joseph the toymaker had passed away in 1729.

The various workshops were probably scattered about the few streets in Bilston but one man, Benjamin, lived 'neare ye heath within the Wolverhampton Liberty'. This was the modern Stowheath Lane and not far from the Ames' workshop at Priestfields. Another man, Joseph, had his home in Ettingshall, on the Sedgley side of the parish boundary near the Mill fields.

Some of the sons carried on the businesses: John Davies took John Tooth to learn toymaking in 1769 at a time when the enamelling trade was flourishing, and Edward, when he died in 1785, was described as a boxmaker. There is no evidence that anyone of this name actually did enamelling work, but plain colouring with the foundation enamel on small boxes may have been done to pass on to the boxpainters and more skilled enamellers for further decoration. On the other hand, the Davies men do not seem to have been property owners nor do their names appear in the trade directories. They worked, like many others in the area, in small workshops, some of them turning out copper shapes for others in the town or neighbourhood to decorate with enamel. There were, doubtless, other workshops in or behind houses, producing boxes, 'toys', hinges, plaques and such items which were handed on to other premises for further treatment. The practice of putting out work and providing the necessary materials for 'home' manfacture, then buying the finished goods, became more prevalent and the evils and hardships which resulted are notable in the case of the nailers in the district.

The value of the register has been made clear throughout, but another factor in trying to find and place actual craftsmen is that, in those days, men were prepared to walk quite long distances to their places of work; the daily journey to Bilston for people living in Wolverhampton, Sedgley, Wednesbury, Darlaston or Willenhall would not be regarded as a hardship. A man might be domiciled in any one of these towns, he and his family being recorded there, but his work or workshop might be in Bilston. One example in reverse is that of William Gibbons who, as early as 1707, was killed in a 'Cole-pitt' in Sedgley parish but his home was in Bilston. Another man who was killed in a pit was Richard Ball in 1728 'by a fall of Coales at Wolverhampton Cole-pitt'.[5]

REFERENCES
[1] W.S.L., Hand Morgan Collection.
[2] S.R.S., 119 Freeholders in County of Staffordshire, p. 264. 1680 Thomas Linton gent. S.R.S., 1923 Hearth Tax Returns 1666, p. 62-64. Thomas Linton, 7 chmineys.
[3] 'Bilston Almanack Sketches 1908', p. 23.
[4] W.S.L., Hand Morgan Collection.
[5] Parish Register, p. 234.

12

THE DECLINE OF THE INDUSTRY

WHEN Queen Victoria ascended the throne in 1837, the enamel trade had become almost extinct and the decline had begun before the close of the eighteenth century.[1]

The most important event had been the great expansion in the coal and iron industries. John Wilkinson, ' Iron-mad Wilkinson ', had established his works in Bilston in 1766,[2] Boulton and Watt were at Soho, near Birmingham, and collieries, blast furnaces, foundries and iron-works were being set up. The face of South Staffordshire was changing rapidly and the semi-rural scene was being transformed into ' The Black Country ' as we know it today.[3]

The historian Shaw writes[4] ' The proprietors of the Hoo estate have lately opened a large colliery of excellent coal, having branches of the Birmingham Canal brought close to it, and there being a quantity of ironstone, Mr. Addenbrook has since erected a large furnace for the purpose of smelting that valuable commodity '. It was near this site that Wilkinson acquired some 23 acres about 1766; a visitor to Bilston in 1790[5] tells how he visited the works and he also describes the town as one of the largest villages in England containing more than a thousand houses. The principal manufactures were ' japanned goods, buckle chapes which are wrought to great perfection, iron screws and recently erected iron furnaces and foundries worked by steam engines '. We do not know how long the visitor stayed, but the fact that no reference is made to the enamelling trade is significant.

Wilkinson became Lord of the Manor of Bradley which was anciently tithe free and long in the possession of the Hoo family. Price says that he established the first forge in Bilston about 1782 and he was himself present when the first ball was put under the hammer.[6]

For business men with capital available, the prospects were unlimited in the new fields of enterprise; one of these was the cutting of the canals to transport coal primarily, then other heavy goods in the South Staffordshire-Birmingham area. In 1767 James Brindley was appointed to make a survey and part of the canal was opened in 1769; it was completed a few years later. Land changed hands frequently. In 1740 the Revd. James Pipe, of the old Bilston family who was then at Chipstead in Surrey, sold to Thomas Tomkys 'all the mines of coal and ironstone and other mines whatsoever in and under the waste lands in the manor of Bradley'. The price was £1,200.[7] Similarly in 1747 John Hoo sold 1/50 share in all his coal-mines and other lands in Bradley. Hoo was very active in this field; a document of the same year refers to payments made by him to John Hicken for drawing up legal documents concerning mines, drainage and so forth.

For low-paid farmworkers, unemployed yeomen and the like there was plenty of work available, hard and dirty though much of it was. They flooded to the area in large numbers; workmen's homes were hastily built in the form of 'courts' or terraces with communal water supply, wash-houses and toilets. Bilston had a 'Newtown', while a short distance away in Bradley a 'Salop Street', or 'Shropshire Row', indicated from whence the majority of the new residents had come. In 1770 the population was a little over 1,000; in 1780 it was a little over 3,000, while by 1811 it had reached 9,646; the 1821 census[8] showed a population of 12,003. It is interesting to observe that of the occupations of the families in the latter returns, 20 were still engaged in farming, 1,980 in trade and 509 in various other pursuits. Four years later the population had reached nearly 14,000. Freeman states that in 1772 there was one blast furnace in Bilston but sixteen in 1818 and in addition, six sheet and bar mills. Writing in about the 1910 period, he declares ' 90 years ago there were over 70 small factories and workshops. Of these 22 were devoted to japanning '.

Lawley tells us that George IV visited Bilston ' incognito ' in 1810. He toured Wilkinson's works (John had died in 1808), went down a pit in the Moorcroft Colliery and took several samples of Bilston industry back to London, including some japanned ware. One might speculate whether some piece of enamel in the royal collection arrived there in this manner.

Obviously some people were doing well out of the industrial boom. One item which shows the increasing prosperity in Bilston is the 'Account of Parochial subscriptions in this County paid into the Bank of England in aid of supplies to H.M. for the Defence of the Nation, 1798 '.[9] Bilston contributed £278.7s.6d. from 117 people. Among the contributors we find members of families mentioned in previous chapters:

> William Bickley—£40.
> Revd. Edward Best—5 guineas annually.
> Joseph Perry, Snr.—5 guineas.
> William Smith Bickley—5 guineas.
> Miss Bickley—1 guinea.
> William Homer—£20.
> Samuel Hanson—5 guineas.
> John Hawksford—2 guineas.
> Richard Hawksford—5 guineas.
> Isaac Beckett—1 guinea.
> William Bickley & Co., Furnacemen—£2.7s.0d.

The varied output by industrial concerns became known far and wide. Pitt in his ' A Topographical History of Staffordshire ' 1817 writes the following: ' Bilston has long been celebrated for its vast mines of coal, ironstone, quarry stone and clay; here are also numerous furnaces for smelting iron ore, forges and slitting mills. It has been asserted that more iron is made in Bilston fields than in the whole kingdom of Sweden '. Much the same descrip-tion appears later in Pigott's Directory of 1829 which states that ' The principal trade carried on here, besides the iron and coal, is japanned and enamelled goods, which are got up in great abundance and cheap '. We have seen, however, that with regard to enamelling, only the Beckett factory is mentioned (Edward's). Under ' Iron and Tinplate Workers and Japanners ' there are 15 names, which include Isaac Beckett of Duck Lane. There are 11 iron founders listed, 14 iron-masters and 4 japanners while two other entries worth noting are Thomas Beckett, lock manufacturer of Bridge Street and Dovey Hawksford, a descendant, screw maker of Lichfield Street. Coal was the all-important commodity in the district being taken from open cast, gin pits and deeper mines. In 1827 the Parish Assessment of coal extracted by various owners was the enormous total of 316,700 tons; it was selling at about 8s.4d. a ton.

Another important factor in the decline of the enamelling

trade was the effect of the French Revolution and subsequent Napoleonic Wars.[10] Not only did industry have to become geared to new and different demands, but the foreign markets were largely lost as Napoleon subdued one country after another and threatened the invasion of England. One aspect of this is seen in the fact that Birmingham, Bilston and other South Staffordshire centres supplied the whole demand for buckles from America, Holland, France, Germany, Italy and Spain. Wolverhampton, in 1792, had many buckle makers and toy makers; in addition there were ten japanners but no enameller listed.

The overthrow of Napoleon at Waterloo in 1815 and the subsequent peace settlement was not the end of the difficulties, for in Bilston, as elsewhere, there followed a period of great depression and unemployment. Men thrown out of work found low-paid jobs in the making of a new straight section of the road from Wolverhampton to Bilston, to be known as Wellington Road after the conqueror of Napoleon, and a section, Oxford Street, was built up to by-pass the old coach route via Bridge Street.

The enamel trade was also to suffer when a change of fashion occurred about 1790. Shoe strings, or laces, were the 'new thing' and the handsome buckles on shoes were no longer in vogue.[11] So serious was the effect felt in Birmingham and South Staffordshire that a deputation went to London to try to see influential people in an attempt to get the trend reversed. Petitions were presented to the Prince of Wales in 1791 and 1792, and Sheridan introduced a deputation of Staffordshire buckle makers to George III. The Duke of York and his duchess forbade the wearing of shoe strings in their household but the tide of change was too strong. Some bucklemakers in Birmingham paraded the town with a donkey, its hooves adorned with shoe strings; people in the streets wearing the hated things were publicly abused and reviled. In 1795 the agitation was still evident, for Pitt was asked to put a tax on slippers and shoe strings. Bucklemakers and enamellers of buckles either had to adapt their work to other forms of production or go out of business.

In London, Bath and other centres where the well-to-do could show off themselves and their wealth there was always an eagerness to follow the 'new thing' or latest craze, particularly if it had royal approval. One such example, towards the latter part

118

of the eighteenth century, was the interest in silhouettes, named after the Frenchman who practised the art of making shadow portraits. George III, Queen Charlotte and their children were keenly interested; Court appointments were made, and professional profilists set up in business in London and the fashionable Spas. Some gifted amateurs produced attractive likenesses and in many homes 'candle pictures' were made. Men like John Miers and Charles Rosenberg and women such as Mrs. Isabelle Beetham had many distinguished sitters; when it is remembered that they were, in a sense, miniaturists, working on bases such as white plaster and glass with attractive mounts, then the counter attraction to the work of the enamellers is obvious.

Another factor to be remembered in connection with the decline is that there was a lasting quality about enamelled objects. Treated with moderate care they maintained their fresh beauty of colour, the bright little pictures remained untarnished; in other words they did not have to be replaced in the way so many modern items need to be. Then again there was always the competition from the ceramic industry. When the fashion of going to the seaside for a holiday spread and was indulged in by more and more people, the need for taking home a little souvenir began to be met by small china objects which probably carried the coat-of-arms and name of the resort, little items to find their place on the mantel-piece or that Victorian piece of furniture known as a 'what-not'.

Finally, in considering the diminution of the enamel trade in Bilston, reference must be made to the developments in industry which led to the application of the basic techniques of enamelling to other purposes, that is in applying enamel to metal sheets, pipes and similar articles as a single colour coating. Painting was replaced by dipping, and later by spraying; artists or box-painters were no longer required.

To conclude this chapter, consideration might be given to the conditions under which the eighteenth century enamellers worked. The earliest of them had small workshops, which might be part of the house itself, or a separate little building at the back. A small workbench, some tools and a muffle furnace were the basic requirements. Later on larger premises were necessary, as in the case of the Bickley establishment, with its reference to a complete room for twenty pair of hands. In Wednesbury three storey buildings were used.

Working conditions must have been very bad; inadequate lighting in winter, the effect of injurious fumes and working with such dangerous items as lead and arsenic without satisfactory ventilation. The application of small amounts of enamel in the exact spots required must have caused great eyestrain to the painters. Hours of work were long and wages low. Some idea of the conditions involved may be obtained from a description given by Hackwood of the contemporary situation in the nail-making industry, another 'home' industry of the area.[12] 'The nail shop is a small, dirty shanty about 12 feet by 10 feet, ventilated only through the doorway and lighted by one or two apertures. Frequently it is adjacent to, and forms part of, the dwelling house of the family of toilers—father, mother and children'. In an 'Essay to Enable the Necessitous Poor to pay Taxes' published in 1713, it was stated that nailers worked from 4 o'clock on Monday morning to late on Saturday to earn three shillings a week.

It would be natural to assume that over the century there would be a marked improvement in working conditions and wages but this was not so. Parliamentary Commissions in 1841 and 1855 stated that 'the lapse or 150 years had neither improved the dwellings, workshops nor habits of a male or female nailer and that the education of their children has continued, till now, to be neglected'. Again, there is a Government Report for 1864 which is very revealing with regard to conditions at that period, and if it is remembered that the people employed in the enamel trade nearly a hundred years earlier would have endured equal, if not worse conditions than the report states, then we can appreciate how hard the daily work was.

Referring to the tinplate and japanning work of 1864 the Report states[13] 'In the smaller factories at Bilston, where the cheaper goods are manufactured, there are about fifty children altogether employed in the painting shops of about 10 to 13 years of age, chiefly girls. Women and girls do the japanning, varnishing and polishing. Women's wages average eight shillings and girls' three shillings and six pence a week . . . In some of the smaller factories at Bilston overtime to 9 and even 11 p.m. is occasionally resorted to for one or two nights in the week, but generally speaking the hours of work are less than in the other trades of the district. The earnings of the children and young persons in the japan factories at Bilston are very small. Boys and girls from 11 to 13 years old get one shilling and six pence to two shillings a week at painting. Girls of 15 get three shillings '.

Young persons in the enamel workshops of around 1785 probably received a little less and an interesting comparison in wages is that with those of the men engaged in cutting the new canals; a labourer in 1796 earned two and six to three shillings a day without beer. It is not surprising that, from time to time, some young apprentice or other employee found work, pay and conditions intolerable and ran away. Those for whom their parents had been obliged to find substantial premiums no doubt completed their apprenticeships, but the boy placed by the Overseers of the Poor with some unsympathetic master till he was 21 years of age might be driven to escape from his servitude as the following notices in ' Aris's Gazette ' prove:—

9th September 1754—' Two apprentices of Joseph Mason, toy-maker, absented themselves '.

10th August 1761—' Whereas Edward Lees, junior, of Bilston, an articled servant to John Parkes of Bilston, bucklemaker, had lately deserted etc.'

2nd November 1761—' John Hartland, apprentice to William Jordan, of Bilston, Chapemaker went away etc.'

8th November 1762—' John Taylor, apprentice to Thomas Ceston of Wolverhampton, buckle maker, absconded etc.'

29th September 1766—' Absconded Charles Griffiths, articled servant to John Bickley of Bilston. Any person employing him after this notice will be prosecuted. Reward.'

The Overseers of the Poor frequently had to place unfortunate boys and girls with masters to learn, supposedly, a trade; when it seemed to them expedient to bind a poor child within their own parish boundaries, then the selected master was obliged to receive him or her whether he wished to or not: not the best beginning to a career in many cases. Because of the frequency with which apprentices absconded, an Act was passed in 1765-1766 which authorised the apprehension and imprisonment of runaway apprentices.

When we see the end-product of the enamellers' art in museums or private collections and admire the beauty and skill involved, we must assume that often they did not reach their finished state without some ' blood, sweat and tears '. Lacking text books, a knowledge of physics, and without electrically-heated and controlled kilns, thermometers, thermostats and other aids, the master enamellers had to rely on their knowledge and experience. They learned from their mistakes and increased in skill and technique from their work and experiments, gradually building up their own notebook of useful knowledge. Of course, much work would be spoiled in the repeated firings and from various other accidents but sufficient fine examples still remain to indicate the high degree of skill and artistry achieved by the Bilston enamellers.

REFERENCES

[1] W. Pitt, ' A Topographical History of Staffordshire ', p. 178-179.
[2] J. A. Langford, ' Staffordshire and Warwickshire Past and Present ', Vol. II Pt. 2, p. 561.
[3] S. Griffith's, ' Guide to the Iron Trade of Great Britain ', 1873, Chapter VI.
[4] S. Shaw, ' History and Antiquities of County of Staffordshire ', Bradley.
[5] Lawley, p. 170.
[6] P. 84. Hackwood, ' Story of the Black Country ', pp. 28-30.
[7] W.S.L., Drift Deeds re Coalmines.
[8] Pitt, ' A Topographical History of Staffordshire ', p. 179.
[9] W.S.L.
[10] G. B. Hughes, ' Battersea and South Staffordshire Enamels ', in ' Collecting Antiques ', p. 72.
[11] J. A. Langford, ' A Century of Birmingham Life ', p. 373.
[12] F. W. Hackwood, ' Story of the Black Country ', pp. 16-18.
[13] Timmins, ' Birmingham and the Midland Hardware District ', pp. 121-4.

13

THE IDENTIFICATION
OF BILSTON ENAMELS

TO assign any particular piece of enamelled ware to Bilston[1] is very difficult and to try to name the individual enameller almost impossible. The objects did not have a monogram or factory mark on them nor carry the initials of the engraver or box painter. We are on safer ground if we attempt to place an enamel within a certain period of time and often this can be estimated from, for example, some royal event of which the date is known, a victory on land or at sea, a political issue of the day, or some incident or personality in the activities of the theatre or sporting world. Not only does this help in eliminating Battersea work if the date is later than 1756, but also that of some enameller when we know the date of his decease.

Attempts have been made to find a clue to some Bilston enamels from their basic colours such as a deep blue, pale pink and pea green, but this is not a reliable test.[2] Reference has been made to one item of undisputed Bilston origin, the Samuel Proud patch box with its transfer-printed lid showing his residence. The lid is not painted but the sides have a rosy pink colour and undoubtedly came from the Isaac Beckett workshop in the period 1770-1780 approximately.

Egan Mew in ' Notes to Illustrations of some Eighteenth Century English Enamels ',[3] 1931, made the following assertions regarding enamels of Bilston origin:—

No. 14—Samuel Proud's box—Beckett Workshop. See Chapter 5.

No. 15—Bickley pieces. See Chapter 6.

No. 23—Small boxes e.g. " Present from Bilston " also six illustrating well known places, six similar from the Warburton Collection in the South Kensington Museum.

Where a private collection has stayed locally in a family, for instance in that of descendants of an enameller, or a collection has has been built up by a local man from his own area,[4] as is said to be the case of a Bilston undertaker, then we are able to give more credibility to statements of origin. Chaffers, in his ' Marks and Monograms on Pottery and Porcelain ', 1912 edition,[5] has some rather disparaging remarks to make about Bilston enamels, considering them to be inferior to Battersea work, but ' still quaint and interesting '. This was before the re-appraisal of London collections. He does have an interesting account of a display of some two thousand enamel patch boxes by a lady ' in whose house they had been stowed away in cases. The history of them is that when manufacturing ceased, or rather failed, in consequence of the changes in fashion, or other causes, about eighty years since, they were taken in lieu of rent by this lady's grandfather; the manufacturer's name was George Brett of Bilston. They were dispersed among the various dealers of London, but these have been absorbed by private collectors '. The lady in question was a descendant of Benjamin Bickley, but that does not prove that either a Brett or a Bickley made any or all of the pieces. Gerald Mander came to the conclusion that it was Miss Laura Bickley to whom reference was made by Chaffers. She was the daughter of John Latty Bickley who was himself the grandson of John and Catherine Bickley. Latty Bickley was something of an eccentric according to Freeman in his ' Black Country Sketches '.[6]

In 1871 Latty Bickley's widow gave some boxes, of not very good quality, to the South Kensington Museum[7] and in the next year she lent a collection which included in addition to boxes, examples of trays, candlesticks, salt cellars and scent bottles. Later these were withdrawn by her daughter, but that lends weight to the possibility that they were Bickley pieces. Gerald Mander, after close examination of these and other collections, tried to reach some conclusions as to characteristic features of Bickley enamels. Possible indications he suggested were:—

Rather crude designs and complicated elaborations and raised work in gold.

Small lightly-stalked sprays of flowers.

A marbling effect achieved by mixing a strong colour with white.

A ' netted ' effect from painting through gauze or muslin. This is found in all the main colours and where over-painting is required the 'net' work is covered over by opaque enamel and the final painting applied.

A debased form of landscape showing heavy towers and snake-like trees.

Large floral sprays with the stalks outlined in black.

Bird and fruit emblems even as early as about 1765-70.

Pretty decoration of more or less single flowers on a raised ground.

Tooled borders gilded and also floral sprays in gilt to accompany the above.

Steel mirrors in lids of boxes usually found instead of glass.

The enamel is extremely soft and easily scratched and broken.

Mander has some comments in the preface to the 1925 Exhibition on the identification of Bilston enamels. He asserts that of the dozens of examples on view, in no instance is a printed transfer found on a 'Bickley' box, but it must be remembered that some doubt has been cast on the origins of many pieces ascribed to the Bickley factory. Mander concluded that pictorial pieces, those for which a transfer has been used and often painted over or, in the better examples, obliterated by beautiful fine work, probably came from the Beckett workshops. He refers to the frequent use of arrangements of rosebuds with other flowers and of blue and yellow colours on a variety of pieces such as étuis, snuff boxes and other items.

Another collection which throws some light on the problem of identification of Bilston enamels was the one described by Egan Mew in an article in 'The Connoisseur' in 1934.[8] This article discussed the enamels collected by Sir Henry Sutcliffe Smith in his search for items associated with Lord Nelson. Mew asserts that a number of these enamels had belonged to 'two members or connections of the two most famous Bilston families—the rival houses of Bickley and Beckett'. If we take the Nelson period to be about 1780-1805, then both Benjamin Bickley and his son John were already dead but John's widow was continuing the business for a time while both Isaac Beckett and his nephew Edward were at work.

In assigning some of the specimens to the Bickley factory, Mew bases his reasons for so doing on the following:—

The character of the transfer printing on the box lids.

The quality of the colouring.

The brilliant, plainly coloured enamel of the lower parts which is ' of that excellent quality which marks it . . . as the product of the Bickley family '.

Some of the subjects illustrated include portraits of the Admiral, one or two ships, naval engagements, commemoration of Trafalgar and the Battle of the Nile (1798) and memorial designs on the death of Nelson. Some boxes have patriotic slogans or couplets, and typical Bilston characteristics include a deep rich blue or pink background and borders of raised white dots; the application of a white base with vertical patterns of blue V's interspersed with a reddish pink spot design is found on the sides of some items. In view of the dates involved, the Becketts would appear to have been the more likely manufacturers of most pieces. There have been exhibitions of enamels at Wolverhampton over the years when pieces were loaned by people who may have known of their origin.

A great deal of research and actual close examination of enamels has been made over the past forty or so years to distinguish between actual Battersea enamels and those from other sources, in particular those from Bilston, Birmingham and Wednesbury.[9] Transfer printed pieces of excellent engraving with fluent, graceful lines and artistic arrangement, having also delicate pale colouring from translucent enamels which do not aim at hiding the lines are features of Battersea work. The lines are clearly delineated and evenly printed.

Plates used at second hand or showing much service gave less sharp and even outlines and so enamels from these came later. They were over-painted in opaque enamels and faults could be hidden by over-painting. Such pieces came from Bilston, and other typical features include raised gilt scroll work, especially on the top of boxes to surround a picture;[10] the use of coloured enamel, other than white, for the background, pale yellow, green or deep blue, for instance; patterns made with raised enamel such as white dots, the criss-cross mesh effect in colour on the surrounds or sides of boxes; the employment of small floral sprays, especially roses and leaves is frequently found, particularly on the sides of boxes; the boxes themselves might have more elaborate shaping, for instance fluted sides and the amusing shapes of the bon-

126

bonnières.[11] Corrugated sides on smaller boxes probably date after 1805 according to Mander.

REFERENCES
[1] F. W. Hackwood, 'Wednesbury Ancient and Modern ', p. 128.
[2] G. B. Hughes, 'Battersea and South Staffordshire Enamels ', in Collecting Antiques ', p. 29.
[3] In Dept. of Ceramics. V. and A. Museum, South Kensington.
[4] J. Freeman, 'Bilston Almanack Sketches ', p. 23.
[5] 3rd Edition, p. 979.
[6] P. 206.
[7] G. B. and T. Hughes, 'English Painted Enamels ', p. 99, and G. B. Hughes, 'Battersea and South Staffordshire Enamels ', in 'Collecting Antiques ', p. 26.
[8] 'The Connoisseur ', Vol. XCIV, pp. 44-49.
[9] B. Rackham, 'Catalogue of the Schreiber Collection ', Vol. III, pp. 26-72, and 'Porcelain as a Sidelight on Battersea Enamels ', T.E.C.C., 1932.
[10] K. Foster, 'Scent Bottles ', p. 54.
[11] G. B. Hughes, 'Battersea and South Staffordshire Enamels ', in Collecting Antiques ', p. 29.

14

OTHER CENTRES OF
ENAMELLING WORK

JUST as buckles were made at other places besides Bilston in
the eighteenth century, in, for example, Birmingham, Wolverhampton, Walsall and Darlaston, so also there were enamellers
at work in Birmingham and Wednesbury. Reference has been
made to the one or two men working closer to Bilston at Sedgley
or Wolverhampton. It will be recalled that as early as 1751
Abraham Seaman of Birmingham was advertising for sale 'all
sorts of colours' which he said were supplied 'to most of the
eminent painters of Birmingham, Wednesbury and Bilston to their
satisfaction'. R. J. Charleston says that Seaman, or originally
Seeman,[1] was of German origin. Several members of this family
were miniaturists and Abraham was an enamel painter in addition
to selling colours. With regard to Wednesbury,[2] the earliest name
is that of Hyla Holden, successively described as boxmaker, box
painter and enameller; it is probable that in Wednesbury enamelling was a development from the earlier trade of pottery. As early
as the reign of Elizabeth I potters are named in the Parish Register.
Dr. Plot records (1686) of Wednesbury, 'divers sorts of vessels
which they paint with Slip, made of a reddish sort of earth gotten
at Tipton '.

Two known potters were Thomas Mills mentioned in a court
case of 1740 and Joseph Perry in land documents of 1749. Other
potters, so described in the Burial Register, were Jonathon Roli-
ston 1744, John Wood, 1766, Thomas Cotton 1783, and Moses
Wood 1784. Colours and glazes would be familiar to these contemporaries of the earliest enamellers in the town and the craft
was practised till the end of the century, though declining before
1800. The Burial Register for the last quarter of the seventeenth
century shows that colliers and nailers were predominant with

some 8 potters and 12 bucklemakers.

The Holdens were an old Wednesbury family; one branch of it worked as nailers and from this branch George died in 1733 and Richard in 1745. Hyla was the son of William and Mary Holden and was born in 1723. His father appears to have been a Church Warden at one time in the parish. Hyla became an apprentice of George Perry in Bilston where he would learn the trade of box-maker and toymaker. If he stayed until he was twenty one, until about 1744, he could have had some knowledge of, or even a little experience in, enamelling. On his return to Wednesbury he set up his own workshop in the Market Place and was soon sufficiently established to take on apprentices. Hyla died in 1766, outlived by his father who died in 1780 at the age of 88 years. Other Holdens contemporary with Hyla include Henry (died 1766), Samuel (died 1764) and John. One or other of these and their children may have done work for Hyla.

In his ' History of Wednesbury ' J. F. Ede[3] writes that Holden took Moses Haughton as an apprentice and that he was probably producing enamelled boxes about 1750. A variation of spelling does not help in trying to trace the family as we have Horton, Aughton and Haughton. A family named Horton appears to have settled in Wednesbury near the end of the seventeenth century, a Gilbert Horton having been a baker in Dudley. He and his wife Rebecca, from nearby Sedgley, had a daughter Mary born at Wednesbury in 1693, and Gilbert's recorded death in August 1713 has the spelling ' Aughton '. The Register has an entry of a son Moses born to Gilbert in 1703 and he married his wife Mary in 1725. There is a Worcester Marriage Licence for April 8th 1723 between Moses Horton of Wednesbury,[4] aged about twenty one and Mary Tibbots of Cradley. They had a son Richard born in 1733 and another, Moses, in 1735 who appears to be the enameller. Hackwood mentions another brother, Matthew, as ' an equally clever painter and engraver ', and we may conclude that there was a successful family business and that the Haughtons had family connections with the Holdens, for William Holden married Mary Haughton, the daughter of Gilbert the baker.

Moses Haughton must have been a good box painter for in 1761 he moved to Birmingham[5] where he joined Henry Clay; his

129

artistic ability was directed to the painting and decorating of japanned and papier-mâché work. The 1781 Directory of Pearson and Rollason mentions ' Moses Haughton—painter, 2 New-market Row '. He must have maintained his interest in enamel painting for between 1788 and 1804 he exhibited thirteen enamels. Later he turned to other art forms and became known for his paintings, particularly of ' still life ' subjects. Bernard Rackham visited Wednesbury during the First World War to examine examples of local enamelling and to talk to interested collectors and enthusiasts. He saw a few pieces in the possession of two old ladies descended from Moses Haughton. The items he was able to examine in Wednesbury included tripod salt-cellars and mustard pots with small landscapes in panels on pink, green or dark blue backgrounds. There is a bust of Haughton in Birmingham Cathedral placed there by his son.[6] During his period in Birmingham he also did work for Baskerville and, like Robert Hancock, he produced a number of engraved plates for the Pearson and Rollason edition of the Bible.[7] He probably returned to Wednesbury for his son, Moses, the younger, was born there about 1772. The visit may have been of a temporary nature for his name appears on a plate in Bisset's ' Poetic Survey Round Birmingham ' 1880, containing the names of Birmingham artists. His son seems to have inherited much of his father's ability, for he, too, became a painter, studying under George Stubbs R.A.[8] and at the Royal Academy, where he later exhibited between 1808 and 1843. He is best remembered however as an engraver. In a correction Ede states that Moses Haughton the Younger was the nephew, not the son, of Moses Haughton the Elder.

The family with the longest connection with the enamelling trade in Wednesbury was that of the Yardleys[9] who, in this respect were similar to the Becketts of Bilston. They operated from Church Street and three generations were engaged in the business, the last being John Yardley who was still manfacturing in 1840. He had inherited from his father Samuel who, in turn, had taken over from his own father Samuel Yardley senior. It has been stated that Yardley senior was the first enameller in Wednesbury but Holden preceded him by over twenty years. He may have set up his business in 1776 when, it is said, he bought the necessary equipment at the Bickley sale in Bilston.

The Yardleys went to Wednesbury from neighbouring Darlaston, for William Yardley and his wife, Susannah Sheldon, are so described when they were married there in 1712, but a Charles Yardley of Halesowen had a son baptized at Wednesbury in 1707. There is a dearth of entries relating to the early Yardleys in the town, but it is probable that William from Darlaston had a son, William, who gave his mother's name to a daughter born to his wife Sarah in 1760. However, it was Samuel Yardley, perhaps another of William's sons, who had a son baptized with the name Samuel in 1776. These two were the enamellers. Samuel senior died in 1794, having been nearly twenty years in the trade.

It is probable that the Yardley premises were more commodious than most in Bilston with better equipment and a larger furnace.[10] They were superior to the old 'workshops' and, in fact, Hackwood speaks of some three-storey buildings which were once enamelling concerns. By 1783 there were at least ten 'enamellers in general' in Wednesbury and some became very prosperous. Samuel Yardley the second was running the business in the time of upheaval in France when the enamelling trade was badly affected, and it is significant that in the 1798 list of 'Parochial Subscriptions for the Defence of the Nation' the only Yardley on the Wednesbury list was William Yardley who contributed three shillings. Samual died in 1806; in the letter of administration he is described as an enameller but his widow's name is given as Ann, whereas Mary was giving birth to his children as late as 1784 when a daughter Eleanor was baptized. The personal estate was sworn at under £100.

It would appear that his son John had more success, extending the business and finding new outlets. In an 1817 directory he is described as an 'enamel box and toy watch maker', the latter did not refer to children's toys but to watches with enamelled faces but no workings. His premises were on Church Hill and he carried on while others closed down, probably ending production himself about 1840. His will, made in 1847, left everything to his son John, who lived in Tewkesbury, and the estate realised under £4,000. He lived for some years after making his will which was not proved till 1860. In it he is called 'gentleman'. Yardley was greatly respected in Wednesbury and for many years he served as High Constable.

Another Wednesbury man who became a successful enameller was James Ross (1745-1821). He is said to have discovered a certain pigment which, in the right proportion, produced a very attractive, delicate shade of pink which was much envied by, and sought after, by all his competitors; it became renowned, not only in England but also abroad. The details of the secret are said to have been obtained unscrupulously, by a rival, from Mrs. Ross while out hunting.

The parish register has entries relating to two burials of 'painters' in successive years, of Thomas Wilkes in 1782 and John Wright in 1783. Though the word 'painter' alone is used, perhaps their artistic skills were at the service of one or more of the local enamellers, although they could have had their own workshops. This would seem to be true in the case of Wilkes for some items in the town collection at Wednesbury were purchased from one of his descendants. With regard to him, Bailey's 'Western and Midland Directory of 1783' mentions a firm of 'Johnson and Wilkes, enamellers in general'. Thomas Dankes was another 'painter' and he may have worked for Hyla Holden at one time for Hyla was a witness at his marriage in 1762 when Dankes was thirty two years of age. Dankes died in 1791.[11]

Other enamellers were Baker, Snape and John Harper. The latter was probably a box painter of some eminence and when the decline in the trade came he turned to portrait painting and engraving. His interest in engraving suggests that he made plates for transfer-printing work.[12] His premises were at Church Hill. Writing about him in 1902, Hackwood described him as a celebrated Wednesbury painter 'whose pictures are in great esteen among local collectors, especially his dead game pieces which are spiritedly drawn and beautifully elaborated and realise from ten to fifty guineas each'. He also engraved plates for William Hawkes Smith's 'Birmingham and its Vicinity' published in 1836. In this reference is made to 'the high ability of one or our artists, Mr. John Harper'. Pearson and Bradshaws' Directory of 1818 describes Harper as an artist. There are several references to the quality of work done by the Wednesbury enamellers.[13] George Alexander Cooke in his 'Complete Itinerary of the County of Staffordshire' claims that 'the enamel paintings are done here to the highest perfection and beauty'.[14] This Pitt reiterated in his

132

'History of Staffordshire' in 1817 when he wrote 'The finest enamel paintings are among the products of its artists'.

The 1818 directory is the one which lists John Yardley as the only enameller and the decline in the trade is a similar story to that at Bilston. The earlier enamellers appear to have purchased most of their metal blanks, boxes, hinges, rims and fittings from Bilston workshops; Bilston mount-turners supplied finely-turned mounts for such items as plaques and medallions. Samuel Yardley, however, made his own mounts and a writer in 'The Times' of 25th of May 1963 gives him the credit for being the first man to copy Meissen bonbonnières in the shape of animals, birds, fruit and the like. He used the dipping method of applying the enamel instead of hand painting, for single colour work, but this does not mark an important advance in technique and could easily have been tried by anyone in the trade.

With a decreasing demand for the popular types of enamelled goods towards the end of the century some Wednesbury men turned to other ways of using their knowledge of the enamelling process. Dr. Sandy Hickling, in 1799, for instance, obtained a patent for enamelling cast-iron and other hollow ware. This type of work made great progress in the nineteenth century and, at Bilston also, this became a well-established industrial form of enamelling. It is worthy of mention that one large factory in Bilston, long engaged in vitreous enamelling, Jordan's, was recently demolished to make way for a re-development scheme, but vitreous enamelling is still important in the area.

The change of attitude towards the eighteenth century products is illustrated by Hackwood who states that as a boy, he saw in 1859, the sale of John Yardley's effects and stock, and several clothes-baskets full of enamels in fine condition were sold to a dealer for a few shillings each basket. They were apparently smashed up in order to obtain the copper bases.[15]

Turning to Birmingham, we find that the connection between bucklemaking, toymaking and enamelling already seen at Bilston is equally applicable here, but on a larger scale. It is probable that in its few years of existence the Battersea factory bought ready made boxes, plaques and such items in blank form from Birmingham manufacturers for the new transfer printing in which it specialised. Hutton, the Birmingham historian wrote, 'The

133

buckle seems to have undergone every figure, size and shape of geometrical invention '. Of the ladies he says: ' It is difficult to discover their beautiful little feet covered with an enormous shield of buckle '.

Buckles and buttons were made from a variety of metals and brass was being manufactured in Birmingham from about 1740. By this time the town was growing rapidly and Samuel Bradford's Survey, published in 1751, indicated that there were 4,170 houses and 23,688 inhabitants, a thorough survey done street by street. Sketchley's Directory of 1767, in a preamble to the list of buckle-makers, states ' An infinite variety are made in White, Yellow, Bath metal, Pinchbeck and Soft White, also of copper and steel, and considering their Beauty and Elegance, the great number of Hands they go through etc. they are bought surprizingly Cheap, and this is the best market for the merchant '. There follows a list of 53 makers, some of whom were toymakers in addition. The list of toymakers runs to 57, while under the heading ' Miscellaneous ' there is an interesting entry: ' Basil Palmer, enamelled Buckle and Button maker '.[16]

Writing of the ' Enamel Manufacturers ' the same directory states: ' These ingenious artists make Candlesticks, Snuff boxes, Inkstands, Tweezers, Toothpick cases, Quadrille Pooles, Smelling bottles, block and Watch faces and all sorts of small trinkets for Ladies Watches etc.' The enamel trade in Birmingham, as in Bilston and Wednesbury, was in being before the Battersea factory was opened and the following advertisements from Aris's Gazette prove this:—

3rd May 1742—Japanned snuff boxes for sale.
14th March 1743—Mr. John Powell, button maker.
7th July 1746—A Box painting business to be let, either with or without shops.
10th August 1747—Henry Barnet ' gilds all sorts of large plates, sword hilts . . . snuff boxes . . . at the lowest price '.
28th September 1747—Enamelled snuff box to be raffled.

Then there are also the three advertisements for the Seaman enamel colours in 1751-1752.

At this point it is important to refer to a man whose work has already been mentioned in connection with Battersea and transfer printing, John Brooks. Bernard Watney and R. J. Charleston have done much research into the early enamelling trade in Birmingham and have shown that as early as September 1751 Brooks was seeking a patent[17]—'the humble petition of John Brooks of Birmingham, in the county of Warwick, engraver, sheweth . . . found out a method of printing, impressing and reversing upon enamel and china from engraved . . . plates. That the said art and method is entirely new and of his own invention'. This petition was not allowed, but the significant fact is the date and the reference to enamel. He made two further unsuccessful attempts when he had moved to Battersea, in 1754 and 1755. The latter claims that Brooks 'can execute curious performances which are pictures themselves, without the help or assistance of the pencil . . . and make a branch of trade which has been hitherto unknown flourish . . . that your petitioner is the first and sole inventor of the aforesaid method of printing on Enamel, China, Glass, Delft and other Wares'.[18]

One man who was an important manufacturer of a variety of articles was John Taylor of whom Hutton reports,[19] 'To this uncommon genius we owe the gilt button, the japanned and gilt snuff boxes at which one servant earned three pounds and ten shillings per week by painting them at a farthing each, that is over three thousand. In his shop were weekly manufactured buttons to the amount of £800 exclusive of other valuable productions'. One member of the nobility for example, purchased, among some articles, 'a toy of eighty guineas value'.

Taylor became High Sheriff of Warwickshire in 1756 and Lady Shelburne gave an interesting account of her visit to his works in 1766.[20] She wrote (May 15th) 'Mr. Taylor, the principal manufacturer there dined with us and we went afterwards to Mr. Bolden's (Boulton's) who trades much in the same way. His house is a very pretty one about a mile out of the town, and his workshops newly built at the end of his garden where they take up a large piece of ground which he has named Soho Square. There, as in the morning, we purchased some watch chains and trinkets at an amazing cheap price . . . We returned home to supper between nine and ten, for we kept early hours. Mr. Baskerville supped with us'. On May 16th she visited Mr. Taylor's 'and he made and enamelled a landscape on the top of a box before us, which he afterwards gave me as a curiosity from my having seen it done. The method of doing it is this, a stamping instrument managed only by one woman impresses the picture on paper, which paper is then laid even upon a piece of white enamel and rubbed hard with a knife or instrument like it, till it is marked upon the box. Then there is spread over it with a brush some metalic colour reduced to a fine powder which adheres to the moist part and, putting it afterwards into an oven for a few minutes, the whole is completed by fixing the colour '. The same day they took tea at Mr. Taylor's villa. 'This is a very handsome house with a dairy and garden about it '. Later still ' Mrs. Baskerville showed us the Japan, which business she has chiefly the management of '.

Lord Shelburne described what he had heard and seen during his own visits, and mentioned that the rapid increase in Birmingham's trade was due to first the discovery of ' mixed metal so mollient or ductile as easily to suffer stamping, the consequence of which is they do buttons, buckles, toys and everything in the hardware way by stamping machines ' and secondly the division of work into various stages with one person doing one stage repeatedly and becoming quick and efficient at it. He said that a button passed through fifty pairs of hands and each could produce a thousand a day. These ' hands ', of course, included those of children.

It is probable that Taylor had used plates engraved by Robert Hancock for some of his better quality products and Eric Benton has pointed out[21] that Brooks and Hancock were both in Birmingham at one period of their lives, when Hancock was serving his apprenticeship there which ended about 1753. He states that, among other items, Brooks produced plates for ' waiters ', japanned trays, for manufacturers such as John Taylor.

John Taylor died in 1775 at the age of sixty four and he had built up a fortune of some £200,000. Together with a Mr. Lloyd he started a bank in Birmingham in 1765, the origin of Lloyds Bank of today.[22] He also purchased Moseley Hall, an estate on the outskirts of the town. Hutton spoke in glowing terms of Taylor calling him ' The Shakespeare or Newton of his day '.

The 1767 directory names four enamellers in Birmingham. Isaac Whitehouse was a manufacturer of snuff boxes (1759) and was later taking apprentices as an enameller and japanner. George

136

Spilsbury as early as 1750 is described as a box painter who, no doubt, bought enamel colours from the Seaman shop in Freeman Street. Also working at this period was John Gibbons, another box painter and another contemporary was Thomas Hunstone who also made buttons. It would appear that Mrs. Seaman had ceased selling enamel colours from her Birmingham shop for her name does not appear in the directory, nor does that of any other supplier, which is rather surprising.

The name of Matthew Boulton is usually associated with that of James Watt in the production of steam engines and the like, but the extensive works at Soho of Boulton and his partner John Fothergill, opened in 1762, produced a great variety of metal items. All types of buttons, buckles, boxes and ornaments were designed and made, and in this field of his activities Boulton was not above taking ideas from the best craftsmen both here and abroad in order to produce beautiful, artistic things. No doubt he was among those Birmingham enamellers and japanners who used engraved plates from the hands of Robert Hancock. But the amount of work being produced in the Birmingham area in japanning, enamelling, and printing meant employment for many artists; John Taylor, giving testimony before a sub-committee of the House of Commons in 1759, asserted that ' There are two or three drawing schools established in Birmingham for the instruction of youth in the arts of designing and drawing and thirty or forty Frenchmen and Germans are constantly employed in drawing and designing '. It should be noted that this was before the later expansion and would account for some relationship with continental styles and fashions.

Matthew Boulton was born in Lichfield in 1728 but his father, who was a silver stamper and piercer, moved to Birmingham. By the age of seventeen Matthew had shown his inventive genius by improved processes for making things like buttons, watch chains and ' toys '. When his father died in 1759, Matthew inherited a thriving business and his marriage in the following year to a Lichfield lady brought him a considerable fortune. Dent[23] writes that when Boulton built his new works at Soho it was to realise his dream to create ' a great industrial college which should train a race of highly skilled workmen and make the manufactures of Soho and the fame of Matthew Boulton honoured the wide world over '. In 1770 he was employing between seven and eight hundred people and some of these were producing enamelled articles of high quality. These figures would include young employees and in addition there would be some work done for Boulton by out-workers and possibly by Bilston and Wednesbury workshops. ' England's Gazeteer ' of 1778 writes of Soho as follows: ' The building consists of four quadrangles, with shops, warehouses etc. for a thousand workmen in the several branches of fabrication of buttons, buckles, etc.'

Mr. J. Bisset, who owned a museum in Birmingham, in 1800 published a ' Poetic Survey Round Birmingham '.[24] It is less poetry than commonplace versifying in rhyming couplets and eulogises everything about the town and its inhabitants as the following extract shows:—[25]

> ' On yonder gentle slope which shrubs adorn,
> Where grew of late, ' rank weeds ', gorse, ling and thorn,
> Now pendant woods and shady groves are seen,
> And nature there assumes a nobler mien,
> There verdant lawns, cool grots and peaceful bow'rs,
> Luxuriant now, are strewn with sweetest flow'rs,
> Reflected by the lake, which spreads below,
> All Nature smiles around—there stands Soho.
> Soho! where Genius and the Arts preside,
> Europe's wonder and Brittania's pride,
> Thy matchless works have raised Old England's fame
> And future ages will recall thy name,
> Each rival Nation shall to thee resign
> The palm of Taste, and own—'tis justly thine,
> Whilst Commerce shall to thee an altar raise,
> And infant Genius learn to lisp thy praise:
> Whilst Art and Science reign, they'll still proclaim
> Thine! ever blended, with a Boulton's name.'

Shaw's ' History of Staffordshire ' has a view of Soho Pool and one of the Soho Factory. The name Soho apparently origi-nated from that of a local inn.

Another figure who became a very successful manufacturer was Henry Clay.[26] At about the age of fifteen he was apprenticed to John Allport of Birmingham, painter, in 1753 for a premium of twenty pounds. The Birmingham Directory of 1777 describes Allport as a ' painter in general ', suggesting that he probably did both enamel and japan work; his name does not appear in the 1781 edition. Clay was established in 1767, according to the Directory for that year, in the firm of Clay and Gibbons which occurs under the list of nine japanners. It appears that japanning interested him more than enamelling, as a short account of him in the Birmingham Weekly Post of 31st January 1890 indicates. This says that Clay was originally an enamel painter but he had a very inventive mind and japanning became his main interest. In 1772 he took out a patent for a special type of paper for doing papier-mâché work for japanning and in 1778 he obtained another patent for making buttons of the same material; he also invented slate buttons and other items.[27] The 1781 directory states: ' Papier-Mâché has here been worked to a texture and consistence so nearly resembling wood in quality and appearance as to deceive persons '. In Bisset's book of 1800 there is an engraved plate the top half of which shows Clay's works, and it has a picture of his newly invented cart. Another plate lists ' Bankers and Gentlemen ' and include:—

> M. Boulton—Soho.
> Sam Lloyd—Crescent East Wing.
> John Taylor—Moseley Hall (His works at Deritend).
> Moses Haughton—Portrait Painter, Dead Game etc.

John Baskerville, another famous Birmingham man who had set up as a japanner in 1740,[28] was the pioneer of the new product, papier-mâché, and Clay learned from him. Baskerville later excelled as a printer. The second Viscount Palmerston visited Birmingham in 1760, mentions Baskerville's printing office and notes of him ' who deals likewise much in japanning '. When members of the nobility or other distinguished persons passed through Birmingham on their travels, it was usual for them to visit one or more of the principal manufactories, principally those of Baskerville, Boulton and Clay.

Dr. Campbell's diary of a visit in 1775[29] has a brief account of Baskerville saying that ' he was originally a little schoolmaster of Worcester, then turned to painter, type founder and printer '. A professed disbeliever in a future state, he gave orders that he should be buried under a mill he had built. Samuel Derrick, who was Master of the Ceremonies at Bath, in a letter to the Earl of Corke in 1767 wrote ' I need not remind your Lordship that Baskerville, one of the best printers in the world, was born in this town and resides near it . . . He manufactures his own paper, types and inks . . . This ingenious artist carries on a great trade in the japan way, in which he showed me several useful articles, such as candlesticks, stands, salvers, waiters, breadbaskets, tea boards etc. elegantly designed and highly finished '.

In his book 'The Making of Birmingham', published in 1893, Dent states that John Baskerville was born at Wolverley in Worcestershire in 1706[30] and became a grave-stone cutter. In 1725 he became a writing master and opened a school in Birmingham Bull Ring, becoming famed for his beautiful handwriting. He later turned to painting on japan ware with premises in Moor Street. When successfully established he turned to the production of a fine form of printing type which later secured his appointment to the University of Cambridge.

Clay's premises were in New Hall (or Newhall Street) and at one time he was employing about three hundred people. He achieved considerable fame and a note in Aris's Gazette of March 26th 1781, recording the death of his wife, describes Clay as 'Japanner to His Majesty'.

Clay found a very satisfactory method of producing with papier-mâché a material as serviceable as wood and he became famed for panels for such things as coach roofs and sides, and sedan chairs.[31] He did such work for the Royal Family and Queen Charlotte had a sedan chair from his workshop; Baskerville had panels from Clay on his own coach. These were japanned and artistically painted and much in vogue. In 1802 Clay moved to London with business premises in King Street, Covent Garden. He died on the 28th of April 1812, leaving a considerable fortune to his three daughters, Elizabeth, Ann and Rebecca. In his will Rebecca is described as 'the wife of Hyla Holden of Birmingham, merchant'. The unusual christian name points to a family connection with the Wednesbury enameller.

Naturally the political and economic changes remarked on in the decline of enamelling and bucklemaking in Bilston were on a bigger scale in Birmingham. Bisset referred to it in his 'Poetic Survey' when he imagines that some of the gods visited the town:—

> 'To see the Buckle Works they next repaired,
> 'Twas ere that Fancy Trade was so impaired,
> When all the Makers had a full employ
> Which made some thousand hearts to dance for joy;
> For Buckles then, by high and low were wore,
> Now were, by Sprigs of Fashion, deemed a ' Bore '.
> A fatal epithet, however gloss'd
> For thousands by that Word, their bread have lost.'

He also gives a glowing account of the workers which is quite biased:—

> 'Inventions curious, various kinds of Toys
> Then occupied the time of men and boys,
> And blooming girls, at work, were often seen,
> That twice their ages joined was scarce fifteen,
> Sent by their parents out, their bread to seek,
> Who'd earn, perhaps, some shillings in a week.'

In the last twenty years of the eighteenth century, Birmingham had far outstripped its neighbours in the variety of its products and the size of its factories and workshops and enamelling was applied to new commercial uses, a development which has continued there to the present day.

REFERENCES
[1] *T.E.C.C.*, 1966.
[2] J. F. Ede, ' History of Wednesbury ', p. 140, later cited as Ede.
[3] P. 140.
[4] F. W. Hackwood, ' Wednesbury Ancient and Modern ', p. 128.
[5] F. W. Hackwood, ' Odd Chapters in the History of Wednesbury ', p. 58.
[6] Ede, p. 140.
[7] F. W. Hackwood, ' Wednesbury Ancient and Modern ', p. 143.
[8] Ibid., p. 140.
[9] F. W. Hackwood, ' Odd Chapters etc.', p. 57.
[10] Ede, p. 140.
[11] F. W. Hackwood, ' Wednesbury Workshops ', pp. 17-19, and F. W. Hackwood, ' Wednesbury Ancient and Modern ', p. 128.
[12] Ede, p. 141. F. W. Hackwood, ' Odd Chapters etc.', p. 58.
[13] Ede, p. 141. F. W. Hackwood, ' Odd Chapters in the History of Wednesbury '.
[14] ' Victoria County History ', Vol. 2, p. 181.
[15] F. W. Hackwood, ' Wednesbury Workshops ', and also in ' Wednesbury Borough News ', 11.4.1925.
[16] Similar list of trades in Pearson and Rollason's Directory, 1780.
[17] Petitions for Patents, *T.E.C.C.*, 1966.
[18] K. Foster, ' Scent Bottles ', p. 50.
[19] R. K. Dent, ' The Making of Birmingham ', p. 218.
[20] ' English Historical Documents ', 1714-1783, ed. D. B. Horn and M. Ransome.
[21] *T.E.C.C.*, 1970.
[22] J. A. Langford, ' A Century of Birmingham Life ', Vol. I, p. 115.
[23] R. K. Dent, ' The Making of Birmingham ', pp. 141-5.
[24] J. A. Langford, ' A Century of Birmingham Life ', Vol. I, p. 197-8, and Vol. II, pp. 144-153.
[25] R. K. Dent, op. cit., p. 370 quotes part of this poem.
[26] C. Gill, ' History of Birmingham ', Vol. I, pp. 99-111.
[27] R. K. Dent, ' The Making of Birmingham ', pp. 145-6.
[28] Ibid., pp. 101-105.
[29] ' Diary of a Visit to England ', Cambridge 1947.
[30] See also V. Bird, ' Portrait of Birmingham ', p. 109.
[31] S. Timmins, ' Birmingham and the Midland Hardware District ', pp. 566-7.

15

EXHIBITIONS OF ENAMELS

FROM time to time there have been held in Wolverhampton exhibitions primarily to display the wide variety of articles made by local industries and some enamel work has been shown.

In 1839 a small, but successful event was organised and a larger exhibition was held in 1840. Japan work was mentioned in the catalogue but not enamel. For the 1869 display Charles Mander loaned some patch boxes and George Wallis, Keeper of Art Collections at the South Kensington Museum, reported as follows:

'Bilston, near Wolverhampton, noted in the last century for its trade in enamelled articles in imitation of Battersea enamels, an industry now extinct in England, has long been the seat of a cheap kind of japanned ware of stamped iron '. He adds that a very good series was exhibited from Bilston.

In 1884 a Fine Arts and Industrial Exhibition was staged and some Bilston enamels were on show; one person loaning items was F. W. Hackwood, the Wednesbury historian already mentioned. In a bedroom display there was an enamelled toilet set, two enamelled vases and a number of Bilston enamelled rings.

The preface to the Old Wolverhampton and District Exhibition of 1925 mentions the valuable work done by Gerald Mander in gathering together and classifying 'the unique collection of Bilston Enamels '. At that time there were no such pieces in the permanent collections of the gallery. In Case 'A' there were items from Mrs. Bantock's collection, some believed to have been purchased about 1880 by Alderman Joseph Jones from a descendant of the maker, Beckett. They agreed with others traced from the same source and, says Mander, are of great assistance in determining the productions of that factory. Etuis and candle-sticks were features of the Beckett pieces.

Case 'B' contained three examples, said to have belonged to Mr. Latty Bickley, from the collection of Clement W. Harris which filled this display. Case 'C' had items from the collection of Mr. Marcus King, then deceased, and one interesting piece was a japanned metal tea-caddy with an enamelled disc inset.

One of the first local men to suggest that Bilston should have a permanent collection of enamels was John Freeman. Writing in the ' Bilston Almanack ',[1] which was published in the first two decades of this century, he wrote ' Let us hope some brilliant youth from the Technical School will re-discover the secret of laying the beautiful enamel copper. May we hint to the Council the wisdom of providing . . . a suitable case for deposit and display of such pieces of Enamel as collectors may be disposed to hand over for the public interest '.

Mr. Gerald Mander was largely responsible for the Exhibition of Bilston Enamels in the Art Gallery November 1943 to January 1944, and again he provided interesting information about them, including the dating of enamels after 1756, when Battersea closed. Among those who loaned pieces were Mrs. Kirk of Wellington Road, Bilston, Mr. Samuel Simeon of Newbridge Crescent, Wolverhampton, Mrs. Wardley of Spring Road, Lanesfield, and Mr. K. H. Lowndes of Sedgley, all local people whose enamels most probably had a Bilston origin.

The most recent, and the most successful exhibition of enamels was that staged at the Wolverhampton Art Gallery in 1973. The absorption of Bilston into Wolverhampton County Borough meant that there were collections of enamels in three places. In Wolverhampton Art Gallery there was a good collection, the basis of Mr. Egan Mew's; in Bantock Park, in the home of a prominent Wulfrunian of that name, was a collection of nearly a hundred items bequeathed to the town by Mrs. Bantock, while in the Bilston Library there was a fine and varied collection which had been built up over the years by gifts and purchases by the Bilston Town Council.

These were brought together for the 1973 exhibition and a comprehensive catalogue of the 670 pieces was prepared by Mrs. Mary Morris, the Assistant Keeper of Applied Arts. In addition to the predominant Bilston enamels there was a wide range of pieces illustrative of the work produced in Battersea, Birmingham,

Wednesbury and Liverpool, each item being described in detail. This collection is now attractively displayed at Bantock Park. It is intended to make a really worthy and permanent exhibition of enamels in Bilston and the gallery has been altered and modernised, under the direction of Mr. David Rogers, the Curator of the Wolverhampton Art Gallery, to show the items at their best.

It is possible, of course, to find collections in other centres. Birmingham has some good examples of enamelled work and at Wednesbury there is a small collection, but in both towns they are not on permanent exhibition. The best examples at Birmingham are some candle-sticks, well made and jointed with all-over patterns in enamel colours and a number of bonbonnières in the form of birds etc. with bright, but not brilliant, colouring in red, brown and yellow. There are two caddies or canisters about 7 inches tall with decorated panels and roccoco scroll work and a patch box has the inscription ' A present from Birmingham '. Manchester and Liverpool possess enamelled pieces, Battersea has a small number but unrepresentative of the finest products of Jansen's factory. There is a collection of enamels in Dudley Museum. In London, the collections most worth seeing are at the Victoria and Albert Museum, in South Kensington, and the London Museum; in both places it is possible to compare the English products with those of other European and Asian origins.

The difficulties in trying with certainty to name the origin of many pieces of enamelled ware have been pointed out and usually only approximate dates of manufacture can be suggested. However this does not prevent the collector, or mere observer, from appreciating the beauty and skilled workmanship seen in so many examples by the eighteenth century enamellers.

REFERENCES
[1] 1908, p. 23.

BIBLIOGRAPHY

Aris's Gazette, Birmingham Reference Library.
Isa Belli Barsali, *European Enamels.*
Samuel Bradford, *A Survey of Birmingham.*
Eric Benton, *Papers Read to the E.C.C.*
J. Bisset, *A Poetic Survey Round Birmingham.*
M. Chamot, *Medieval Enamels.*
W. Chaffers, *Marks and Monograms on Pottery and Porcelain.*
R. J. Charleston, *Papers Read to the E.C.C.*
C. Cook, *The Art of Robert Hancock,* T.E.C.C.
C. Cook, *The Life and Work of Robert Hancock.*
G. A. Cook, *A Complete Itinerary of the County of Staffordshire.*
H. Cunynghame, *European Enamels.*
Prof. R. K. Dent, *The Making of Birmingham.*
R. Dossie, *The Handmaid of the Arts,* 1758.
F. Ede, *History of Wednesbury.*
The Encyclopedia of World Art.
W. & B. Forman, *Limoges Enamels.*
Kate Foster, *Scent Bottles.*
H. Malcolm Fraser, *The Staffordshire Domesday.*
John Freeman, *Black Country Sketches.*
John Freeman, *Bilston Almanack Sketches.*
John Freeman, *Wesleyan Methodism in Bilston.*
Griffiths, *Guide to the Iron Trade of Great Britain.*
F. W. Hackwood, *Wednesbury Workshops.*
F. W. Hackwood, *Wednesbury Ancient and Modern.*
F. W. Hackwood, *Odd Chapters in the History of Wednesbury.*
F. W. Hackwood, *Oldbury and Round About.*
C. Hadfield, *The Canals of the West Midlands.*
W. B. Honey, *Old English Porcelain.*
G. B. Hughes, *Collecting Antiques.*
G. B. Hughes, *English Snuff Boxes.*
G. B. Hughes, *Battersea and South Staffs. Enamels.*
G. B. and T. Hughes, *English Painted Enamels.*
W. H. Jones, *The Story of the Japan and Tinplate Working in Wolverhampton.*
J. A. Langford, *A Century of Birmingham Life.*
G. T. Lawley, *A History of Bilston.*

145

Lewis and Day, *Enamelling*.
Gerald Mander, *The Wolverhampton Antiquary*.
Gerald Mander, *Transcripts of Apprentices Lists*, (MSS).
Gerald Mander with N. Tildesley, *A History of Wolverhampton*.
Egan Mew, *Notes on Illustrations of some 18th Century English Enamels*.
Connoisseur, Vol. XCIV, *Bilston Memorials of Nelson*.
Oxford University Press, *History of English Arts*.
A. Pasquin, *An Authentic History of Painting in Ireland*.
W. Pitt, *A Topographical History of Staffordshire*.
Dr. R. Plot, *The Natural History of Staffordshire*.
J. Price, *An Historical Account of Bilston*.
B. Rackham, *Catalogue of the Schreiber Collection*.
G. Reynolds, *English Portrait Miniatures*.
R. Sayer, *The Artist's Vade Mecum*, 1776.
Stebbing Shaw, *History and Antiquities of the County of Staffordshire*.
S. Smith, *Birmingham and its Vicinity*.
Samuel Timmins, *Birmingham and the Hardware District*.
A. J. Toppin, *Papers Read to the E.C.C.*
W. Turner, *Transfer Printing on Enamels, Porcelain and Pottery*.
The Victoria, *History of Staffordshire*.
G. C. Williamson, *Portrait Miniatures*.
R. Turner Wilcox, *The Mode in Footwear*.
Susan Benjamin, *English Enamel Boxes*.
Mary Morris, *Catalogue of English Painted Enamels*.

INDEX